Looking at Teaching Through the Lens of the FFT Clusters

Study Guide
Set 1

The Danielson Group
contact@danielsongroup.org

Contents

Study Guide Overview

Introduction

Welcome to the FFT (Framework for Teaching) series of Clusters Study Guides. Their purpose is to guide professional learning communities as they engage in activities and discussions to enhance their own practices and the practices of their colleagues. An Instructional Set of lesson artifacts (that may include lesson plans, a video of the entire lesson, student work, and teacher commentary) is used as a resource for each Study Guide. The combination of the Study Guide activities, the Instructional Set artifacts, and the user's experience yields a powerful method of examining teaching and applying learning to one's own practice.

Background

The Instructional Sets are actual lessons led by teachers with their own students. The videos run the duration of the lesson. The teachers and students are not actors, and the lessons are part of their curriculum, not something that was scripted for the Study Guides. The Danielson Group is extremely appreciative of the teachers and their students for providing an opportunity for others to view authentic classroom artifacts for the purpose of professional growth.

A team of educational practitioners and Danielson Group consultants, who have extensive experience in effective teaching practices and professional development training, created this Study Guide series (see Appendix A for the team members). The team received rigorous training on the FFT

Clusters and on how to analyze the teaching and learning evident in the Instructional Sets. They worked with Charlotte Danielson, lead consultants, and each other to create the contents of the Guides.

The series includes many Study Guides. Each Guide was written for a group of accompanying Instructional Sets. The collection includes a sampling of K–12 lessons in Mathematics, English Language Arts, Science, Social Studies, and Science Technology. The majority of lessons are in Mathematics and English Language Arts. Analyzing lessons from a variety of grades and subject areas provides opportunities for educators to stretch their analytic skills and enhance their understanding of the FFT Clusters. A list of the Instructional Sets can be found in Appendix B.

The team created a Record of Evidence for each Instructional Set. The activities portion of the Study Guide provides highlights of the Instructional Set, whereas the Record provides an extensive list of evidence gleaned from the video and artifacts for the FFT Clusters. A Record also includes interpretations of the evidence by the authors who were trained as coders. For each Record, two coders analyzed an Instructional Set independently, then compared their records to produce a composite version for the Study Guide. The Record of Evidence does not contain scores or evaluations, since the evidence is intended for use in professional conversations.

Contents of the Study Guides

Each Study Guide provides a multi-step process for examining the contents of an Instructional Set, reflecting on and discussing its contents, and applying learning from such study to new situations. Each Guide provides the following steps:

Step 1: Lesson Overview

This section provides a high-level summary of the lesson, culled from the video, lesson plans, and artifacts, to provide readers with some background information about the Instructional Set. Many include pre-observation notes in addition to the lesson plans. All lessons are based on rigorous student standards such as the Common Core State Standards (CCSS)/ College and Career Readiness Anchor (CCRA) Standards.

Step 2: Preparation and Questions

Users examine artifacts that the teacher provided as evidence of preparing the lesson. The planning artifacts in an Instructional Set will include the lesson plans and related artifacts such as student assignments, if appropriate. Examining the planning artifacts and jotting down what to look for will help prepare users for viewing the video of the classroom lesson. Users will also generate questions that they have about the artifacts and use those questions when discussing the lesson with their colleagues.

Step 3: Viewing the Classroom Video

Users view the video of the full lesson and note significant behaviors of the teacher and students. Some of the Instructional Sets include samples of student work. The samples were selected by the teacher and do not include teacher comments. If student work is included, users will review it after viewing the video.

Step 4: Selected Highlights of the Lesson Video

This step provides a summary of important teacher and student behaviors that happened in the lesson, and which aspects of the teaching and learning are being exemplified. These noteworthy behaviors will provide users with a lens for their examination of the lesson with their colleagues, and an opportunity to match the highlights with the FFT Clusters.

Step 5: Viewing the Teacher Commentary

Users watch the video of the teacher commentary about the lesson and the students, and jot down noteworthy information. A summary of the commentary and its relationship to effective aspects of teaching are provided.

Step 6: Questions, Applications, and Discussion

Prompts are provided that guide users in analyzing and reflecting on the Instructional Set. This step also includes a set of prompts for thinking about applications to a user's own practice.

Using the Study Guides

The power of professional learning comes when educators can have focused discussions about the teaching and learning that they witness. Individuals can use the Study Guides, but the process of discussing with colleagues what one has learned from the Instructional Set, and how it can be applied to one's own practice, is the action needed to enhance teaching and learning. Just watching videos of effective teachers is not enough to change practice. Additional thinking and actions are needed to effect change. Therefore, the Study Guides are intended for use by educators participating in professional learning communities.

The Guides can be used in any order, but it is recommended that users begin with a grade level and subject area with which they are comfortable.

There are two versions in each Study Guide: one for communities of teachers and one for communities of instructional coaches or mentors of teachers. The first five steps of the process are identical in both versions, and are designed to focus on examining the instruction. A group setting is not necessary for Steps 1–5. They can be completed at an individual's own pace.

Steps 1–5 could be completed as a whole group, though this is not recommended, since interaction is not part of these steps. Watching a 45-minute video is usually best done as an individual activity so the viewer can control the pacing and the volume or elect to wear headphones.

Step 6 requires participants to share their responses, observations, suggestions, and other insights. It is highly recommended that participants work in small groups, so all get an opportunity to contribute to the discussions. The facilitator could select highlights of the small group discussions to share with the whole group.

Step 6 is a group activity, focusing on analyses of the Instructional Set and applications of learning. The activities in Step

6 are similar in the two versions, but the discussions will be different in subtle ways because of the user's role.

Teachers	Instructional Coaches
Communities with all teachers will analyze and reflect on the Instructional Set in Step 6 and will identify an aspect of the learning that went well and another aspect that could be improved. Their colleagues in the community will discuss the analyses and suggest teaching techniques to support student learning as related to the featured lesson. After that activity, the teacher community will think about what they learned from the teacher and lesson, and how they might apply that learning to their own teaching.	*Communities with all coaches/mentors will analyze the Instructional Set in Step 6 and discuss how to prepare for a conversation with the featured teacher. Their colleagues in the community will discuss the analyses and planned questions, comments, and suggestions. Step 6 includes an activity that has the coaches thinking about what they learned from the teacher and lesson, and how they might apply it to their own coaching situation.*

There may be communities comprising educators with different roles, such as a combination of teachers, teacher leaders, and a mentor of beginning teachers. The prompts in Step 6 can be easily modified to accommodate their different roles. There also might be situations where the professional development is done in a whole group setting. Just as with the mixed group learning communities, the prompts and implementation can be modified to support the professional development of all participants.

The Study Guides should be treated as one possible way of using the Instructional Sets for professional growth among educational colleagues. The Guides do not advocate any particular model of coaching or professional learning. If practitioners have a certain model that is used in their district, then they should consider modifying Step 6 to meet their needs or requirements. Additional prompts or steps can be included to support their learning and accommodate their schedules.

Post-Study Activities

Learning communities are encouraged to use the Study Guides as a springboard for creating their own additional professional development activities.

The following example shows an additional set of prompts that could be completed after the learning community completes the activities in Step 6 of the Guide. It serves as a reflective activity and should be done by individuals, then shared with their colleagues.

Here's What, So What, Now What

  a. *Here's What:* Identify five takeaways from your conversations with your colleagues. What examples did you collect?

  b. *So What:* How do your takeaways connect to your current practice?

  c. *Now What:* Based on the takeaways, identify 1–3 next steps you will take to inform your future practice.

Connection to the FFT Clusters

The Study Guides provide information and instructions on how to examine teaching and learning through the lens of the Framework for Teaching (FFT) Clusters. There are three versions of the FFT Clusters document: Generic, Literacy (ELA), and Mathematics. The Generic version reflects those instructional practices that are common across disciplines and was used for these Study Guides. The Literacy and Mathematics versions translate the general language of the narratives and critical attributes, where appropriate, into content-specific language.

Steps 1, 4, and 5 (lesson overview, lesson highlights, and teacher commentary) contain specific information about the Instructional Set and include prompts to match evidence to the related FFT Clusters. It is strongly suggested that copies of the FFT Clusters be available for participants so they can use them during their work with the Study Guides.

Even though the Guides were created with the FFT Clusters in mind, they also can be used to examine the Instructional Sets through the lens of the components of the Framework for Teaching. Practitioners who are familiar with the Framework for Teaching components will find the crosswalk between the Clusters and the components useful. It is located at the beginning of the FFT Clusters document. The FFT Clusters document can be downloaded for free individual use from the Danielson Group website: www.danielsongroup.org.

If practitioners use a different set of teaching standards than the Framework, they will still find the Study Guides and Instructional Sets useful for their professional growth needs. A crosswalk between their teaching standards and the FFT Clusters should be done so practitioners can associate the evidence in the Instructional Sets with their own standards.

Before you begin your examination of an Instructional Set's materials, you may want to check your equipment to make sure you can access the video and artifacts included with the Instructional Set. Enjoy studying the teaching and learning in the Instructional Set, and be prepared to enhance your own practice.

Looking at Teaching Through the Lens of the FFT Clusters

A Study Guide for
Teacher
Learning Communities

Teacher: Gee
Subject: ELA
Grade: 8th
Topic: Science Literacy:
The Manhattan Project

Welcome to the Study Guide for the Gee English Language Arts Instructional Set, a collection of artifacts and videos for an instructional lesson. This Study Guide provides information and instructions on how to examine teaching and learning through the lens of the Framework for Teaching (FFT) Clusters. In order to complete the steps in this Guide, you will need access to the teacher's planning documents, the lesson video, and the teacher commentary video (http://www.danielsongroup.org/study-guides/). This Study Guide has been designed so Steps 1–5 focus on examining the Instructional Set, and can be done by an individual. Step 6 is a group activity and focuses on proposed interactions with the featured teacher and applications of learning.

Step 1 - Lesson Overview

Read the background information of the lesson provided below.

Students read along with the teacher in this science literacy lesson, and highlight information in the article "The Manhattan Project" by Sam Roberts. The lesson is aligned to the Common Core standards, with the focus on:

- citing specific text evidence to support analysis of science
- providing an accurate summary of the text
- reading and comprehending science/technical texts

Prior to this lesson, the basics of atomic theory have been discussed. Learning the basics of atomic theory provides background knowledge to today's current understanding of atoms and molecules.

The lesson is aligned to the following CCSS standards:

- RST.6-8.1: Cite specific textual evidence to support analysis of science and technical texts.
- RST.6-8.2: Determine the central ideas or conclusions of a text; provide an accurate summary of the text distinct from prior knowledge or opinions.
- RST.6-8.10: By the end of grade 8, read and comprehend science/technical texts in the grades 6-8 text complexity band independently and proficiently.

Students find direct evidence from the text, using questions that are text-based. Students read the article to determine answers to these questions:

1. Why was the Manhattan project a secret to the general public as well as men in government?

2. Why did the Manhattan Project take place in New York City? What was special about this location?

3. In the article it states, "Supplies of uranium were secured, and secret factories were built to process it. Speed was essential." Why did they think that speed was essential? Was speed really important?

4. After reading the first three paragraphs in the "Fat Man and Little Boy" section of the article, find the sentence that best demonstrates the secrecy of the project.

The lesson plan identifies student worksheets that will be collected and reviewed individually as a means of assessing how well the students responded to the questions using direct evidence from the text.

Mr. Gee's lesson plan includes specific formative assessment (Five-question Socrative formative assessment, if time permits).

Step 2 - Preparation and Questions

- *Read the teacher's lesson plan and jot down the key things you expect to see and what you want to look for in the video of the lesson.*
- *Write down any questions or comments you have about the lesson plan.*

Artifacts included:
- Lesson plan
- "The Manhattan Project" article by Sam Roberts
- Student worksheet
- Reflection video with Steve Gee
- Samples of student work

Step 3 – Viewing the Classroom Video

- *Watch the video of the entire lesson, noting those things you expected to see based on the lesson plan.*
- *Note what was missing based on your expectations from the lesson plan. Jot down significant behaviors of the teacher and students pertinent to the FFT Clusters.*
- *After watching the video, look at the samples of student work provided (if available).*

Step 4 – Selected Highlights of the Lesson Video

This science literacy lesson is a teacher-led discussion about an article students are reading. Teacher reads aloud "The Manhattan Project" by Sam Roberts. Students read along with the teacher, and highlight information in the article. Students find direct evidence from the text to answer four teacher-created questions (see questions listed in Step 1).

Read the highlights of the lesson provided below. Note those matching your highlights of the lesson. For each set of statements, determine the FFT Cluster that is best related to the behaviors presented.

> A. Mr. Gee conveys expectations for students by having them read along and highlight information that is important in the article, "The Manhattan Project." His explanation of the content consists of a lecture with participation by students. (Cluster ___)
>
> B. The classroom displays posters, a calendar, class schedules, and has a SMART Board. Classroom is arranged in two groups of tables, with 12 desks per group. Students and teacher can move around the classroom. The physical environment of the classroom supports the instructional goals and learning activities. (Cluster ___)

C. Mr. Gee stands in the center of the classroom, pauses at various points of time during the reading of the article, and asks some text-dependent/text-specific questions. Students review each question, highlight evidence from the text, share thinking with a neighbor (in a " Think-Pair-Share" strategy), and respond as a whole group to each question on the SMART Board. The teacher asks students to explain their reasoning and cite specific evidence. (Cluster ____)

D. Mr. Gee monitors student learning while students review their work individually. He provides feedback to individual students as he circulates in the room. An assessment section is included in the lesson plan, identifying student worksheets that will be collected and reviewed individually to see how well the students did at responding to the questions with direct evidence from the text. Time is allotted for students to complete the worksheet. The student worksheets are distributed at the end of the lesson to complete as homework. (Cluster ____)

Step 5 – Viewing the Teacher Commentary

Watch the video of the teacher's commentary about the lesson and jot down any questions or comments you have about the commentary. Read the highlights below and identify the related FFT Cluster.

A. Mr. Gee notes that prior to this lesson, the basics of atomic theory have been discussed. Mr. Gee decided to introduce a literacy component to tie in the reading informational texts, so he searched for an article that was challenging but interesting. Mr. Gee states "What better way to engage the students than by introducing them to bombs and explosions." He also shares that talking about the atomic bomb is beneficial to future planning and connects to the students' history lessons. (Cluster ___)

B. This science literacy lesson focuses on the Reading Common Core standards that deal with the complexity of the text. Students find direct evidence from the text using questions that are text-based. Students read the article to determine their answers. Mr. Gee believed the" big push" was getting the students into the text and not relying on their background knowledge. Teacher-created questions require students to read for understanding. (Cluster ___)

C. Mr. Gee acknowledges the Common Core standards shifts and makes a concerted effort to include more challenging texts, more reading, and hands-on activities. Those shifts are addressed in today's lesson. Prior to the Common Core standards, Mr. Gee states he would not have spent this much time in reading an article and creating text dependent questions that prevent students faking their way through the activity. He states he "likes the kids doing science but is making a big push this year (every quarter) to introduce an article, have students do some reading." Students respond to text-based questions and learn from each other while working and talking with their peers. (Cluster ___)

D. Mr. Gee wants everyone in the class to participate in the activity; the Think-Pair-Share instructional strategy supports this focus. He notes that collaborations between students are encouraged when he pauses; students are required to talk to their neighbor and bounce ideas back and forth. He believes this strategy supports students who are struggling; "talking and hearing other students' opinions helps." (Cluster ___)

Step 6 – Activities for Teacher Learning Communities

The purpose of this step is to prompt your analysis and reflection of the Instructional Set and to have you think about applications to your own practice.

1. Teaching and Learning Related to the FFT Clusters

The purpose of this activity is to increase your understanding of the relationship between the highlights of the Instructional Set and the FFT Clusters. Your responses to the identification of an FFT Cluster to each of the highlights in Steps 4 and 5 is compared to the responses by the master coders. The Answer Key is located at the end of the activities. You have options on how to complete the comparison. Determine what might work best for your group's learning. You may want to design your own activity to check and discuss the match between highlights and the FFT

Clusters. Some suggested options include, but are not limited to the following:

- Look at the first set of highlights. Take a poll of what each group member identified as the related FFT Cluster. If all members said the same FFT Cluster, have one or two members say why. Compare the group's response to the answer sheet. Repeat for the remainder of the highlights.

OR

- Have each member take one or two highlights. State the correct answer for each one, and a reason why the highlight demonstrates that FFT Cluster. The member will facilitate a discussion if others had different responses, with the goal of having all understand the justification of the correct answer.

OR

- Have members check their own responses to all the highlights. If there are any incorrect answers, then the member selects one highlight and leads a discussion with the group to learn why others think the highlight matches the correct FFT Cluster.

OR

- Determine your own process to check and discuss the match between highlights and the FFT Clusters.

2. **Analysis and Reflection of the Instructional Set**

The purpose of this activity for you to analyze and reflect on what you saw and heard in the artifacts and videos, to share your analysis with your peers, and to discuss some of the questions or comments you noted. Review the notes, comments, and questions you recorded when you examined the Instructional Set.

- Identify a key teaching and learning attribute demonstrated in the Instructional Set that was effective and state why you think it worked well.
- Identify a different attribute and provide ideas about how it could be enhanced or improved.
- Share your statements with your group and have your peers react to and build upon your analysis and ideas.

Sample statements:

I noticed both in the lesson plan and also in the commentary that the teacher has been trying to include a written text in his lessons. He made an intentional effort to incorporate instructional strategies to engage students in the activity, "Think, Pair, Share." Students were grouped for small group work. The entire class would have benefited from more probing questions and responses, because understanding the "Manhattan Project" was important work. I would suggest having each student pair with another student to share each other's understanding of the assigned reading and to determine their response to teacher-created questions.

Additional ideas for statements:
- Degree that the instructional strategies, scaffolding, and materials and resources align with the goals and are appropriate for these students
- Extent to which the learning environment is safe for risk taking, and how that environment is established and maintained
- Extent to which students demonstrate a commitment to mastering challenging content. You know your students. Which students did you see persevere well in their

research? Which students do you believe could have demonstrated a little more persistence? Can you think of a strategy you might try in the future to encourage their persistence when you observe some students quitting or giving up when met with challenges?

- Extent that teacher monitored student understanding and methods used

3. **Notice, Learn, and Apply**

The purpose of this activity is for you to reflect on what you learned from your analysis of the Instructional Set and to determine how you will apply it to your teaching.

- Complete the statements:
  "I noticed _____."
  (Insert one thing you noticed about the teacher or students.)

  "And I learned _____."
  (State what you learned related to what you noticed.)

  "I will apply what I learned by _____."
  (Provide example of how you will use what you learned in your own context.)

- Share your statements with your group. Have others react and add how they might apply what you noticed to their own teaching context.

Sample statements:

- I noticed the teacher had the students do a Think-Pair-Share at their table groups, sharing their thinking about teacher-created open-ended questions.
- I learned that students need prompts to begin the conversation, challenge their thinking, and make connections.

- I will apply what I learned during this science literacy lesson when challenging students' thinking and making connections to previous readings and discussions across various content areas.

Study Guide for Teachers Answer Key

Highlights from the
Lesson Video
(Step 4)

A. Mr. Gee conveys expectations for students by having them read along and highlight information that is important in the article, "The Manhattan Project." His explanation of the content consists of a lecture with participation by students. (Cluster 2: Safe, Respectful, Supportive, and Challenging Learning Environment)

B. The classroom displays posters, a calendar, class schedules, and has a SMART Board. Classroom is arranged in two groups of tables, with 12 desks per group. Students and teacher can move around the classroom. The physical environment of the classroom supports the instructional goals and learning activities. (Cluster 3: Classroom Management)

C. Mr. Gee stands in the center of the classroom, pauses at various points of time during the reading of the article, and asks some text-dependent/text-specific questions. Students review each question, highlight evidence from the text, share thinking with a neighbor (in a " Think-Pair-Share" strategy), and respond as a whole group to each question on the SMART Board. The teacher asks students to explain their reasoning and cite specific evidence. (Cluster 4: Student Intellectual Engagement)

D. Mr. Gee monitors student learning while students review their work individually. He provides feedback to individual students as he circulates in the room. An assessment section is included in the lesson plan, identifying student worksheets that will be collected and reviewed individually to see how well the students did at responding to the questions with direct evidence from the text. Time is allotted for students to complete the worksheet. The student worksheets are distributed at the end of the lesson to complete as homework. (Cluster 5: Successful Learning by All Students)

Study Guide for Teachers Answer Key

Highlights from the
Teacher Commentary
(Step 5)

A. Mr. Gee notes that prior to this lesson, the basics of atomic theory have been discussed. Mr. Gee decided to introduce a literacy component to tie in the reading informational texts, so he searched for an article that was challenging but interesting. Mr. Gee states "What better way to engage the students than by introducing them to bombs and explosions." He also shares that talking about the atomic bomb is beneficial to future planning and connects to the students' history lessons. (Cluster 2: Safe, Respectful, Supportive, and Challenging Learning Environment)

B. This science literacy lesson focuses on the Reading Common Core standards that deal with the complexity of the text. Students find direct evidence from the text using questions that are text-based. Students read the article to ascertain their answers. Mr. Gee believed the" big push" was getting the students into the text and not relying on their background knowledge. Teacher-created questions require students to read for understanding. (Cluster 3: Classroom Management)

C. Mr. Gee acknowledges the Common Core standards shifts and makes a concerted effort to include more challenging texts, more reading, and hands-on activities. Those shifts are addressed in today's lesson. Prior to the Common Core standards, Mr. Gee states he would not have spent this much time in reading an article and creating text dependent questions that prevent students faking their way through the activity. He states he "likes the kids doing science but is making a big push this year (every quarter) to introduce an article, have students do some reading." Students respond to text-based questions and learn from each other while working and talking with their peers. (Cluster 4: Student Intellectual Engagement)

D. Mr. Gee wants everyone in the class to participate in the activity; the Think-Pair-Share instructional strategy supports this focus. He notes that collaborations between students are encouraged when he pauses; students are required to talk to their neighbor and bounce ideas back and forth. He believes this strategy supports students who are struggling; "talking and hearing other students' opinions helps." (Cluster 5: Successful Learning by All Students)

**Looking at Teaching Through
the Lens of the FFT Clusters**

A Study Guide for
Instructional Coach
Learning Communities

Teacher: Gee
Subject: ELA
Grade: 8th
Topic: Science Literacy:
The Manhattan Project

Welcome to the Study Guide for the Gee English Language Arts Instructional Set, a collection of artifacts and videos for an instructional lesson. This Study Guide provides information and instructions on how to examine teaching and learning through the lens of the Framework for Teaching (FFT) Clusters. In order to complete the steps in this Guide, you will need access to the teacher's planning documents, the lesson video, and the teacher commentary video (http://www.danielsongroup.org/study-guides/). This Study Guide has been designed so Steps 1–5 focus on examining the Instructional Set, and can be done by an individual. Step 6 is a group activity and focuses on proposed interactions with the featured teacher and applications of learning.

Step 1 - Lesson Overview

Read the background information of the lesson provided below.

Students read along with the teacher in this science literacy lesson, and highlight information in the article "The Manhattan Project" by Sam Roberts. The lesson is aligned to the Common Core standards, with the focus on:

- citing specific text evidence to support analysis of science
- providing an accurate summary of the text
- reading and comprehending science/technical texts

Prior to this lesson, the basics of atomic theory have been discussed. Learning the basics of atomic theory provides background knowledge to today's current understanding of atoms and molecules.

The lesson is aligned to the following CCSS standards:

- RST.6-8.1: Cite specific textual evidence to support analysis of science and technical texts.
- RST.6-8.2: Determine the central ideas or conclusions of a text; provide an accurate summary of the text distinct from prior knowledge or opinions.
- RST.6-8.10: By the end of grade 8, read and comprehend science/technical texts in the grades 6-8 text complexity band independently and proficiently.

Students find direct evidence from the text, using questions that are text-based. Students read the article to determine answers to these questions:

1. Why was the Manhattan project a secret to the general public as well as men in government?

2. Why did the Manhattan Project take place in New York City? What was special about this location?

3. In the article it states, "Supplies of uranium were secured, and secret factories were built to process it. Speed was essential." Why did they think that speed was essential? Was speed really important?

4. After reading the first three paragraphs in the "Fat Man and Little Boy" section of the article, find the sentence that best demonstrates the secrecy of the project.

The lesson plan identifies student worksheets that will be collected and reviewed individually as a means of assessing how well the students responded to the questions using direct evidence from the text.

Mr. Gee's lesson plan includes specific formative assessment (Five-question Socrative formative assessment, if time permits).

Step 2 - Preparation and Questions

- *Read the teacher's lesson plan and jot down the key things you expect to see and what you want to look for in the video of the lesson.*
- *Write down any questions or comments you have about the lesson plan.*

Artifacts included:

- Lesson plan
- "The Manhattan Project" article by Sam Roberts
- Student worksheet
- Reflection video with Steve Gee
- Samples of student work

Step 3 – Viewing the Classroom Video

- *Watch the video of the entire lesson, noting those things you expected to see based on the lesson plan.*
- *Note what was missing based on your expectations from the lesson plan. Jot down significant behaviors of the teacher and students pertinent to the FFT Clusters.*
- *After watching the video, look at the samples of student work provided (if available).*

Step 4 – Selected Highlights of the Lesson Video

This science literacy lesson is a teacher-led discussion about an article students are reading. Teacher reads aloud "The Manhattan Project" by Sam Roberts. Students read along with the teacher, and highlight information in the article. Students find direct evidence from the text to answer four teacher-created questions (see questions listed in Step 1).

Read the highlights of the lesson provided below. Note those matching your highlights of the lesson. For each set of statements, determine the FFT Cluster that is best related to the behaviors presented.

> A. Mr. Gee conveys expectations for students by having them read along and highlight information that is important in the article, "The Manhattan Project." His explanation of the content consists of a lecture with participation by students. (Cluster ___)
>
> B. The classroom displays posters, a calendar, class schedules, and has a SMART Board. Classroom is arranged in two groups of tables, with 12 desks per group. Students and teacher can move around the classroom. The physical environment of the classroom supports the instructional goals and learning activities. (Cluster ___)

C. Mr. Gee stands in the center of the classroom, pauses at various points of time during the reading of the article, and asks some text-dependent/text-specific questions. Students review each question, highlight evidence from the text, share thinking with a neighbor (in a " Think-Pair-Share" strategy), and respond as a whole group to each question on the SMART Board. The teacher asks students to explain their reasoning and cite specific evidence. (Cluster ___)

D. Mr. Gee monitors student learning while students review their work individually. He provides feedback to individual students as he circulates in the room. An assessment section is included in the lesson plan, identifying student worksheets that will be collected and reviewed individually to see how well the students did at responding to the questions with direct evidence from the text. Time is allotted for students to complete the worksheet. The student worksheets are distributed at the end of the lesson to complete as homework. (Cluster ___)

Step 5 – Viewing the Teacher Commentary

Watch the video of the teacher's commentary about the lesson and jot down any questions or comments you have about the commentary. Read the highlights below and identify the related FFT Cluster.

A. Mr. Gee notes that prior to this lesson, the basics of atomic theory have been discussed. Mr. Gee decided to introduce a literacy component to tie in the reading informational texts, so he searched for an article that was challenging but interesting. Mr. Gee states "What better way to engage the students than by introducing them to bombs and explosions." He also shared that talking about the atomic bomb is beneficial to future planning and connects to the students' history lessons. (Cluster ___)

B. This science literacy lesson focuses on the Reading Common Core standards that deal with the complexity of the text. Students find direct evidence from the text using questions that are text-based. Students read the article to determine their answers. Mr. Gee believed the" big push" was getting the students into the text and not relying on their background knowledge. Teacher-created questions require students to read for understanding. (Cluster ___)

C. Mr. Gee acknowledges the Common Core standards shifts and makes a concerted effort to include more challenging texts, more reading, and hands-on activities. Those shifts are addressed in today's lesson. Prior to the Common Core standards, Mr. Gee states he would not have spent this much time in reading an article and creating text dependent questions that prevent students faking their way through the activity. He states he "likes the kids doing science but is making a big push this year (every quarter) to introduce an article, have students do some reading." Students respond to text-based questions and learn from each other while working and talking with their peers. (Cluster ___)

D. Mr. Gee wants everyone in the class to participate in the activity; the Think-Pair-Share instructional strategy supports this focus. He notes that collaborations between students are encouraged when he pauses; students are required to talk to their neighbor and bounce ideas back and forth. He believes this strategy supports students who are struggling; "talking and hearing other students' opinions helps." (Cluster ___)

Step 5 – Viewing the Teacher Commentary

Watch the video of the teacher's commentary about the lesson and jot down any questions or comments you have about the commentary. Read the highlights below and identify the related FFT Cluster.

A. In the teacher reflection video, Mr. Gee notes that prior to this lesson, the basics of atomic theory have been discussed. Mr. Gee decided to introduce a literacy component to tie in the reading informational texts, so he searched for an article that was challenging but interesting. Mr. Gee states "What better way to engage the students by introducing them to bombs and explosions." He also shared that talking about the atomic bomb is beneficial to future planning and connects to the students' history lessons. (Cluster ___)

B. This science literacy lesson focuses on the Reading Common Core standards that deal with the complexity of the text. Students find direct evidence from the text using questions that are text-based. Students read the article to ascertain their answers. Mr. Gee believed the" big push" was getting the students into the text and not relying on their background knowledge. Teacher-created questions require students to read for understanding. (Cluster ___)

C. Mr. Gee acknowledges the Common Core standards shifts and makes a concerted effort to include more challenging texts, more reading, and hands on activities. Those shifts are addressed in today's lesson. Prior to the Common Core standards, Mr. Gee states he would not have spent this much time in reading an article and creating text dependent questions that would prevent students faking their way through the activity. He states "he likes the kids doing science but is making a big push this year (every quarter) to introduce an article, have students do some reading." Students respond to text-based questions while working and talking with their peers, learning from each other. (Cluster ___)

D. Mr. Gee wants everyone in the class to participate in the activity; the Think-Pair-Share instructional strategy supports this focus. He notes that collaborations between students are encouraged when he pauses; students are required to talk to their neighbor and bounce ideas back and forth. He believes this strategy supports students who are struggling; "talking and hearing other students' opinions helps." (Cluster ___)

Step 6 – Questions, Applications, and Discussion

The purpose of this step is to prompt your analysis of and reflection on the Instructional Set and to have you think about applications to your own practice.

1. **Preparation for professional conversation with the featured teacher**

The purpose of this activity is to increase your understanding of the relationship between the highlights of the Instructional Set and the FFT Clusters. Your responses to the identification of an FFT Cluster to each of the highlights in Steps 4 and 5 is compared to the responses by the master coders. The Answer Key is located at the end of the activities. You have options on how to complete the comparison. Determine what might work best for your group's learning. You may want to design your own activity to check and discuss the match between highlights and the FFT Clusters. Some suggested options include, but are not limited to the following:

- Look at the first set of highlights. Take a poll of what each group member identified as the related FFT Cluster. If all members said the same FFT Cluster, have one or two

members say why. Compare the group's response to the answer sheet. Repeat for the remainder of the highlights.

OR

- Have each member take one or two highlights. State the correct answer for each one, and a reason why the highlight demonstrates that FFT Cluster. The member will facilitate a discussion if others had different responses, with the goal of having all understand the justification of the correct answer.

OR

- Have members check their own responses to all the highlights. If there are any incorrect answers, then the member selects one highlight and leads a discussion with the group to learn why others think the highlight matches the correct FFT Cluster.

OR

- Determine your own process to check and discuss the match between highlights and the FFT Clusters.

2. **Analysis and Reflection of the Instructional Set**

The purpose of this activity for you to analyze and reflect on what you saw and heard in the artifacts and videos and discuss some of the questions or comments you noted. This activity provides you and your peers the opportunity to practice preparing questions to get more information about the teacher's thinking and the behaviors of both the students and the teacher, which is one element of a professional conversation. The feedback from your peers about your questions should include to what extent they are appropriate and will obtain useful information without making the featured teacher feel uneasy or criticized. The second part of this activity focuses on helping teachers move their practice forward. Please note that having you prepare for and model an entire conversation about the lesson with the featured teacher is not the purpose of this activity as written. Your group can modify or replace the activity to meet your group's needs.

- Review the notes, comments, and questions you recorded when you examined the Instructional Set. Pretend you have the opportunity to ask the teacher some questions to get additional information about the strategies used or decisions made for this Instructional Set.

- Next, think of what you would say to prompt the teacher's thinking about how to enhance their practice. Share with your group just the questions you would use with the teacher to elicit additional information. Have your peers comment about your questions and add other questions they had about the same event.

- Share with others in your group what you would do to prompt the teacher's thinking and actions to enhance his/her practice. Take turns sharing and discussing the prompts.

Sample A:

Part 1 – You stated that you want everyone in the class to participate in the lesson. You planned the Think-Pair-Share instructional strategy to support this focus, since collaboration between students encourages them to talk to their neighbor and bounce their ideas back and forth. You believe this strategy supports students who are struggling: "talking and hearing other students' opinions helps." It appears that the students looked to you to orchestrate their interactions. What scaffolds might you put in place so that students might begin to respond to each other without your intervention?

Part 2 – What knowledge or skill might these and other students need in order for them to be able to facilitate the discussion? What knowledge, skill, or attitude might you need to teach so that all students might be able to facilitate the discussion? What might you as a teacher use as criteria to determine when you might need to interject?

Sample B:

Part 1 – You demonstrated the importance of participation in this lesson. Given the procedures you taught prior to the lesson, what did you notice that students were doing well, and/or what procedures might need some additional practice? What specific student actions might demonstrate that they responded to one another's work?

Part 2 – What might you do to prompt and support student grouping, student thinking, and discussion as you return to the process of group participation and gathering information in tomorrow's lesson? What does "deeper exploration" look/sound like to you with regards to this specific lesson? What do you pay attention to that signals when it is a good time to transition into deeper exploration? What criteria might be used to discern when transitioning would be appropriate? What are some strategies you might use to initiate that transition?

3. **Notice, Learn, and Apply**

The purpose of this activity is for you to reflect on what you learned from your analysis of the Instructional Set and to determine how you will apply it to your coaching.

- Complete the statements:

   "I noticed _____."
   (Insert one thing you noticed about the teacher or students.)

   "And I learned _____."
   (State what you learned related to what you noticed.)

   "I will apply what I learned by _____."
   (Provide example of how you will use what you learned in your own context.)

- Share your statements with your group. Have others react and add how they might apply what you noticed to their own coaching context.

Sample statements:

- I noticed that Mr. Gee's lesson did not provide the opportunity for students to be self-directed; only a few students responded to one another's ideas.
- I learned that teachers need to model those procedures so that students understand how they can self-direct their learning.
- I coach some teachers to plan for modeling and demonstration opportunities, in readings and discussions across various content areas, to support students in self-directed learning. I will also try to use student self-direction when addressing issues as I coach teachers.

Study Guide for Instructional Coaches Answer Key

Highlights from the
Lesson Video
(Step 4)

A. Mr. Gee conveys expectations for students by having them read along and highlight information that is important in the article, "The Manhattan Project." His explanation of the content consists of a lecture with participation by students. (Cluster 2: Safe, Respectful, Supportive, and Challenging Learning Environment)

B. The classroom displays posters, a calendar, class schedules, and has a SMART Board. Classroom is arranged in two groups of tables, with 12 desks per group. Students and teacher can move around the classroom. The physical environment of the classroom supports the instructional goals and learning activities. (Cluster 3: Classroom Management)

C. Mr. Gee stands in the center of the classroom, pauses at various points of time during the reading of the article, and asks some text-dependent/text-specific questions. Students review each question, highlight evidence from the text, share thinking with a neighbor (in a "Think-Pair-Share" strategy), and respond as a whole group to each question on the SMART Board. The teacher asks students to explain their reasoning and cite specific evidence. (Cluster 4: Student Intellectual Engagement)

D. Mr. Gee monitors student learning while students review their work individually. He provides feedback to individual students as he circulates in the room. An assessment section is included in the lesson plan, identifying student worksheets that will be collected and reviewed individually to see how well the students did at responding to the questions with direct evidence from the text. Time is allotted for students to complete the worksheet. The student worksheets are distributed at the end of the lesson to complete as homework. (Cluster 5: Successful Learning by All Students)

Study Guide for Instructional Coaches Answer Key

Highlights from the
Teacher Commentary
(Step 5)

A. Mr. Gee notes that prior to this lesson, the basics of atomic theory have been discussed. Mr. Gee decided to introduce a literacy component to tie in the reading informational texts, so he searched for an article that was challenging but interesting. Mr. Gee states "What better way to engage the students than by introducing them to bombs and explosions." He also shares that talking about the atomic bomb is beneficial to future planning and connects to the students' history lessons. (Cluster 2: Safe, Respectful, Supportive, and Challenging Learning Environment)

B. This science literacy lesson focuses on the Reading Common Core standards that deal with the complexity of the text. Students find direct evidence from the text using questions that are text-based. Students read the article to ascertain their answers. Mr. Gee believed the" big push" was getting the students into the text and not relying on their background knowledge. Teacher-created questions require students to read for understanding. (Cluster 3: Classroom Management)

C. Mr. Gee acknowledges the Common Core standards shifts and makes a concerted effort to include more challenging texts, more reading, and hands-on activities. Those shifts are addressed in today's lesson. Prior to the Common Core standards, Mr. Gee states he would not have spent this much time in reading an article and creating text dependent questions that prevent students faking their way through the activity. He states he "likes the kids doing science but is making a big push this year (every quarter) to introduce an article, have students do some reading." Students respond to text-based questions and learn from each other while working and talking with their peers. (Cluster 4: Student Intellectual Engagement)

D. Mr. Gee wants everyone in the class to participate in the activity; the Think-Pair-Share instructional strategy supports this focus. He notes that collaborations between students are encouraged when he pauses; students are required to talk to their neighbor and bounce ideas back and forth. He believes this strategy supports students who are struggling; "talking and hearing other students' opinions helps." (Cluster 5: Successful Learning by All Students)

Record of Evidence

This Record of Evidence (ROE) contains key evidence aligned to the FFT Clusters. Interpretive statements about the evidence are also provided. The ROE was created by two master coders who recorded evidence and interpretation statements independently, reviewed each others' work, and arrived at a final composite version based on their professional conversations. This version was reviewed by a leader of the master coders. The ROE is included in this Study Guide so users can see what master coders identified as key evidence, and their interpretation of that evidence through the lens of the FFT Clusters. It is provided as an example of one type of analysis of an Instructional Set. The ROEs were created for professional development rather than evaluative purposes. Users are cautioned about using them for teacher evaluation.

Rubric:	Generic
Grade:	8th
Subject:	ELA
Topic:	Science Literacy: The Manhattan Project
Teacher description:	Male, caucasian
Class description:	26 regular education students total; no SpEd; no ELL Students
Artifacts:	• Lesson plan • Teacher commentary • Student worksheet
Length of video:	39:40

Cluster 1: Clarity of Instructional Purpose and Accuracy of Content

Guiding Questions

- *To what extent does the teacher demonstrate depth of important content knowledge and conduct the class with a clear and ambitious purpose, reflective of the standards for the discipline and appropriate to the students' levels of knowledge and skill?*

- *To what degree are the elements of a lesson (the sequence of topics, instructional strategies, and materials and resources) well designed and executed, and aligned with the purpose of the lesson?*

- *To what extent are they designed to engage students in high-level learning in the discipline?*

Record of Evidence

Evidence

Instructional Plan
- Teacher provided a lesson plan listing lesson objective, the Literacy Common Core Standards addressed, class demographics, Anticipatory Set, required materials, text usage information, procedures, primary core action indicators, assessment, and follow up.
- Lesson is aligned to standards with the focus on citing specific text evidence to support analysis of science, providing accurate summary of the text, reading and comprehending science/technical texts.

Artifacts
- Lesson plan
- New York Times Upfront article, "The Manhattan Project" by Sam Roberts
- Student worksheet
- Dry erase boards and markers for the Think-Pair-Share activity

Interview

00:00-03:03
- The teacher notes that prior to this lesson, they have discussed the basics of atomic theory. Teacher decided to introduce a literacy component to tie in the reading information texts, so searched for an article that was challenging and interesting. "What better way to engage the students than by introducing to them to bombs and explosions?" Teacher stated that talking about the atomic bomb is essential to future planning and to connect to their history lessons.
- Teacher states that the CCSS focus in this lesson deals with the complexity of the text and students can find direct evidence from the text using questions that are text-based. Students are to read and find the information in the article to determine their answers. Big push was getting the students into the text and not use their background knowledge. Questions require students to read for understanding.

3:03-5:41
- Teacher acknowledges the CCSS shifts and makes a concerted effort to include more challenging texts and include more reading. This lesson addresses those shifts. Prior to the CCSS, teacher would have not spent this much time in reading an article, creating questions that were designed to be text dependent so that students could not fake their way through….teacher states that he likes the kids doing science but is making a big push this year (every quarter) to introduce an article, have students do some reading, respond to text base questions, and work and talk with their peers, thus learning from each other.
- Teacher wants everyone in the class to participate in the activity. Mr. Gee uses the Think-Pair-Share strategy to support this focus.

Record of Evidence

Cluster 1: Clarity of Instructional Purpose and Accuracy of Content

Evidence (cont'd.)

5:42
- Teacher states that the most noticeable student behaviors noted in this lesson was exemplified in Core Action 3. "The collaboration between the students was noticed when I would pause, students were required to talk to their peers and bounce their ideas back and forth. This supports students who are struggling, as it gets the students talking and hearing other students opinions, which helps."

Video

00:00-4:00
- T: Today we are going to have a little discussion about an article we are going to read. I am going to read it aloud, discuss it as we go, and the title of the article is "The Manhattan Project."
- Teacher asks opened-ended questions.
- T: Anybody have any clues what this is going to be about? A few people.
- T: Seth what is your guess? (Student responds.)
- T: What does Manhattan means to you?
- T: Drew, what do you think?
- Drew: I actually know what it is.
- T: Some good ideas. It is about the development of the first atomic bomb. The reason I chose this article is twofold. We are in the middle of atomic theory discussion. Think back to your timeline. Do you remember what our understanding of atoms represent? Why theory? Not law? Not fact?
- Teacher connects the article to the students' learning in history that they are studying.
- T: Around Christmas, you will be getting into World War II era; when the atomic bomb was developed.

4:01-4:56
- T: I am going to read the article out loud.
- Teacher passes out the article.
- T: Use pen or highlighter for some important information.
- Teacher states three questions that he wants students to think about as he is reading the article.
- The teacher displays three main concepts while reading on the SMART Board:
  - Secrecy of the project?
  - Location of the project?
  - The speed at which the project was completed?

Record of Evidence

Cluster 1: **Clarity of Instructional Purpose and Accuracy of Content**

Evidence (cont'd.)

05:17
- T: This is a challenging article.
- T: I am going to pause several times as we read it, sometimes about the vocabulary and sometimes to ask questions that I want you to be thinking about. Please follow along with me.
- Students are seated in desks in two groups (12 in each row). Two students seated on side of room at individual desks.

Interpretation
- Teacher Commentary, lesson plan, teacher artifacts, and student work are helpful for an observer to understand the teacher's thinking.
- The purpose for today's lesson was shared in the teacher video interview, lesson plan, and at the beginning of the classroom video.
- Depth of important content knowledge is demonstrated by completing the three standards noted for this lesson. Additionally, the teacher conducts the class with clear expectations, reflective of the standards. Questions posed appear appropriate for students to answer with text-based evidence.
- There is little evidence to show that the teacher understands why the CCSS are important for this concept/topic in science. There are no science standards included in the lesson plan.
- Although the teacher intends for the students to share their rationale for their answer, the teacher typically calls on one student and then is done.

Record of Evidence

Cluster 2: Safe, Respectful, Supportive, and Challenging Learning Environment

Guiding Questions

- *To what extent do the interactions between teacher and students, and among students, demonstrate genuine caring and a safe, respectful, supportive, and also challenging learning environment?*

- *Do teachers convey high expectations for student learning and encourage hard work and perseverance? Is the environment safe for risk taking?*

- *Do students take pride in their work and demonstrate a commitment to mastering challenging content?*

Evidence

01:14
- T: Seth what is your guess? Student responds.
- T: What does Manhattan means to you?
- T: Drew what do you think?
- Drew: I actually know what it is.
- Teacher conveys modest expectations for students by having them read along and highlight information that is important in the article, "The Manhattan Project." The teacher's explanation of the content consists of a monologue, with minimal participation or intellectual engagement by students.

5:58
- T: Please follow along with me.
- Teacher begins reading the article. Teacher reads and then stops to ask students a question about the meaning of the phrase.

6:54
- T: What do you think the phrase nuclear annihilation means? Annihilation is a big word, lots of syllables, lots of vowels.

7:10
- Some students raise their hands.
- S: Destruction.

3:55-4:15
- Little instructional time lost in transition from whole group work to individual work.
- Teacher passes out articles to students while continuing to talk about the article, displaying the three big main concepts on the SMART Board. Students immediately take a copy of the article and pass down to the next student.
- Most students have a pen or highlighter and are writing as teacher reads the article.

Record of Evidence

Cluster 2: **Safe, Respectful, Supportive, and Challenging Learning Environment**

- Planned learning tasks, materials, and question sequences support the lesson's purpose; they are well sequenced and are suitable for most students in the class.
- Lesson plan identifies text usage information, indicating that the selected article, "The Manhattan Project" is a reading level of 9th-10th grade. Teacher states that this is a challenging but interesting article chosen for the lesson (teacher video and classroom video).

05:17
- T: This is a challenging article.
- T: I am going pause several times as we read it, sometimes about the vocabulary and sometimes to ask questions that I want you to be thinking about. Please follow along with me.

Interpretation
- The overall interactions between teacher and students and between student and student is respectful and supportive.
- The students' pride in their work and commitment to mastering the challenging content is questionable.
- It is somewhat difficult to discern high levels of cognitive energy.
- Students seem to be somewhat hesitant to answer questions in front of the entire class.
- The teacher has high expectations for students in some respects, but in others, such as reading aloud to the students, expectations seem low.
- The Lesson Plan section identifies all 3 Core Action Indicators that will be visible in the lesson.

Record of Evidence

Cluster 3:   Classroom Management

Guiding Questions

- *Is the classroom well run and organized?*

- *Are classroom routines and procedures clear and carried out efficiently by both teacher and students with little loss of instructional time?*

- *To what extent do students themselves take an active role in their smooth operation?*

- *Are directions for activities clearly explained so that there is no confusion?*

- *Do students not only understand and comply with standards of conduct, but also play an active part in setting the tone for maintaining those standards?*

- *How does the physical environment support the learning activities?*

Evidence

- The classroom is observed to have posters, calendar, class schedules and SMART Board. Classroom arrangement grouped in two groups of tables: 12 desks to a group. Students and teacher could move around the classroom.
- Student behavior is appropriate during the entire lesson.

4:11
- Teacher hands out the article
- T: You should have a 2 page article.

17:23
- (Four) students shown in the video don't seem to know who their partners are. They are all talking to one another. The girl in pink is talking across the table to the girl in white. The boy with the gray hoodie is not talking to anyone. He then joins in the conversation and they give a high-five across the table.
- Students seem to be unclear as to who their partners are. There are some pairs, some singles, a group of six. One pair is called upon, because they are talking about something other than the article. The boy (Garcia?) reads directly from the article, the teacher asks, "Why?" He can not answer and the teacher goes immediately to another student.
- Teacher is giving directions as students are packing up, ready to leave the classroom.
- Transition from whole group to individual work is smooth, as students begin to read silently for two minutes.

16:57
- T: Take a couple minutes to share with your neighbor why you think it was a secret and provide your evidence.

Record of Evidence

Cluster 3: Classroom Management

- 17:10
- Students begin immediately to pair and share.
- Teacher circulates around the room, checking for students' understanding. Teacher is able to circulate around two rows of 12 desks and the two desks located on the side of the classroom.
- The teacher is giving directions as students are packing, up ready to leave the classroom.

Interpretation
- There seems to be confusion about partners for the discussion. By the time the pairs get formed, there seems to be insufficient time to have deep conversations about the questions.
- It is not known if the students had an active part in creating the standards of conduct.
- The physical environment of the classroom appeared to support the instructional goals and learning activities.
- The teacher commentary video expands on Core Action 3, describing student behaviors.
- The teacher uses the strategy of questioning to get groups re-engaged with the task. When one group is called upon and cannot answer, the teacher does not hold them accountable.

Record of Evidence

Cluster 4:   Student Intellectual Engagement

Guiding Questions

- *To what extent are students intellectually engaged in a classroom of high intellectual energy?*

- *What is the nature of what students are doing?*

- *Are they being challenged to think and make connections through both the instructional activities and the questions explored?*

- *Do the teacher's explanations of content correctly model academic language and invite intellectual work by students?*

- *Are students asked to explain their thinking, to construct logical arguments citing evidence, and to question the thinking of others?*

- *Are the instructional strategies used by the teacher suitable to the discipline, and to what extent do they promote student agency in the learning of challenging content?*

Evidence

- Teacher stands in the center of the classroom and asks the four questions; students review each question, highlight evidence from the text, share thinking with neighbor, and respond in whole group with text evidence to the each question on the SMART Board:

Q1. Why was the Manhattan project a secret to the general public as well as men in government? Provide evidence from the text.
- T: Two minutes to think about it. Two minutes to share.
- Students work individually for two minutes silently highlighting and then share with neighbor their evidence for two minutes.
- Teacher uses open-ended questions and scaffolds for new learning.
- T: What does The Manhattan Project mean to you? (Gets students to predict.)
- S: I already know what it is. It's when they built the atomic bomb.
- T: Why is it called atomic theory instead of law?
- Teacher explains the difference between theory and law.

4:23
- T: I want you to keep these 3 main concepts in your head as I'm reading this article.

5:56
- Teacher begins reading the article.

Record of Evidence

Cluster 4:   Student Intellectual Engagement

Evidence (cont'd.)

6:48
- Most students are at least looking at their article, none are seen highlighting or underlining. One boy (in blue) is doing something with his palm.
- T: What do you think nuclear annihilation means? Big word lots of syllables, lots of vowels.
- Two hands are seen raised, the teacher calls on one of the students.
- T: Based on what we've read so far....why do you think nuclear weaponry put in doubt the survival of civilization?
- Student answers.
- T: So, expand....

9:10
- T: Could be harnessed, what does harnessed mean? (Calls on one student after a pause.)

11:50
- T: What would be the author's intent with 'in theory?'

14:15
- Teacher puts a question on the board and verbally gives directions as to what the students should do (the question and "provide evidence" are on the screen.)
- T: You have about 2 minutes.
- He clarifies what is to be done with 3 different students.

18:10
- T: who is willing to share? Why is this secret? Please provide a piece of evidence.
- Students respond: (quote from Hitler).
- T: So assuming this is all true... published on the front page? Why do we care about this?
- Students respond.
- T: Obviously the threat of Germany.

Q2. Why did the Manhattan Project take place in New York City? What was special about this location? Provide evidence from the text.

Q3. In the article it states, "Supplies of uranium were secured, and secret factories were built to process it. Speed was essential." Why did they think that speed was essential? Was speed really important? Provide evidence from the text.

Q4. After reading the first three paragraphs in the "Fat Man and Little Boy" section of the article, find the sentence that best demonstrates the secrecy of the project.

Record of Evidence

Cluster 4: Student Intellectual Engagement

- The teacher asks students to explain their reasoning and cite specific evidence, but only some students attempt to do so.

27:30
- About half the students participate in the whole group discussion as ten students raise their hands, responding to teacher questions.

39:19
- T: I am going to pass out a handout that has four questions, which three we have discussed. Your homework: take your direct evidence and we will talk about your responses tomorrow.
- Teacher provides 32 minutes for group/small work.
- Small group work ends and transitions into a rushed closure of the lesson.

Interpretation
- High levels of energy and enthusiasm by many students was not observed.
- Some students are intellectually engaged at some points during the lesson. However, the teacher takes one student's response and then summarizes what that one student has said. The other students wait and listen for the summary of the teacher.
- As the teacher is reading, the students' only direction is to "keep these 3 main concepts in your head."
- Although the questions are at higher levels of thinking and not requiring one right answer, not all students are intellectually engaged. The teacher accepts one student's answer and then summarizes for the class. There is no discussion, only recitation between the teacher and the student who is called upon.

Record of Evidence

Cluster 5:   Successful Learning by All Students

Guiding Questions

- *To what extent does the teacher ensure learning by all students?*

- *Does the teacher monitor student understanding through specifically designed questions or instructional techniques?*

- *To what extent do students monitor their own learning and provide respectful feedback to classmates?*

- *Does the teacher make modifications in presentations or learning activities where necessary, taking into account the degree of student learning?*

- *Has he or she sought out other resources (including parents) to support students' learning?*

- *In reflection, is the teacher aware of the success of the lesson in reaching students?*

Evidence

- "What did I say the atomic number represented?"
- Teacher monitors by walking between the tables.
- A student responds to the question posted, but the answer does not really answer the question. Teacher says, "If this were a test that would be a very good answer, but would it answer this question?"

20:21
- T: Let me ask this question another way…what is some proof in that first part that it was kept secret?

24:11
- Teacher stops to direct a student who is not reading.
- T: I'm going to give you a worksheet to finish as homework.

33:44
- Teacher circulates around the room, using proximity to check the understanding of individual students and of group thinking.
- Teacher uses open-ended questions to check for student understanding as teacher reads article to whole group.

Q1. Why was the Manhattan project a secret to the general public as well as men in government? Provide evidence from the text.

Q2. Why did the Manhattan Project take place in New York City? What was special about this location? Provide evidence from the text.

Record of Evidence

Cluster 5:   Successful Learning by All Students

Evidence (cont'd.)

Q3. In the article it states, "Supplies of uranium were secured, and secret factories were built to process it. Speed was essential." Why did they think that speed was essential? Was speed really important? Provide evidence from the text.

Q4. After reading the first three paragraphs in the "Fat Man and Little Boy" section of the article, find the sentence that best demonstrates the secrecy of the project.

- An assessment section is included in the lesson plan, stating students worksheet would be collected and reviewed individually to see how well the students did at responding to the questions with direct evidence from the text. Time does not permit the students to complete the worksheet. The students worksheets are distributed at end of the lesson for students to complete as homework.
- Lesson plan includes specific formative assessment (5- question Socrative formative assessment, if time permits). Time did not permit for this planned formative assessment.

Interpretation
- The teacher monitors student learning while students review their work individually, but teacher feedback to individual students as teacher circulated the room can not be heard.
- Modifications in the observed lesson or the inclusion of parents as additional resources for the lesson are not observed.
- Teacher record keeping is not observed in the lesson or in the artifacts.
- The teacher's reflection how the lesson could be improved is not observed.
- Planned 5-question Socrative formative assessment is not observed, as time did not permit.
- Students are dependent upon the teacher for knowing if they have the answer correct or not. All monitoring is between the teacher and the students.
- There seems to be some confusion in the questions, as the teacher has to frame the question a different way than what was originally stated.
- Other than changing the question, the lesson seems to follow an expected timeline; the teacher says that they are going to have to take the rest to do as homework, because of the reading task.

Record of Evidence

Cluster 6: **Professionalism**

Guiding Questions

- *To what extent does the teacher engage with the professional community (within the school and beyond) and demonstrate a commitment to ongoing professional learning?*

- *Does the teacher collaborate productively with colleagues and contribute to the life of the school?*

- *Does the teacher engage in professional learning and take a leadership role in the school to promote the welfare of students?*

Evidence

No evidence of Cluster 6 is present in this Instructional Set.

**Looking at Teaching Through
the Lens of the FFT Clusters**

A Study Guide for
Teacher
Learning Communities

Teacher: Penney
Subject: Mathematics
Grade: 3
Topic: Perseverance, Solving
Using Different Strategies

Welcome to the Study Guide for the Penney Math Instructional Set, a collection of artifacts and videos for an instructional lesson. This Study Guide provides information and instructions on how to examine teaching and learning through the lens of the Framework for Teaching (FFT) Clusters. In order to complete the steps in this Guide, you will need access to the teacher's planning documents, the lesson video, and the teacher commentary video (http://www.danielsongroup.org/study-guides/). This Study Guide has been designed so Steps 1–5 focus on examining the Instructional Set and can be done by an individual. Step 6 is a group activity and focuses on proposed interactions with the featured teacher and applications of learning.

Step 1 - Lesson Overview

Read the background information of the lesson provided below.

This lesson is an application of what students have been learning about multiplication. The teacher states that she uses real-world problems to help students make connections from the math they are learning in school to what is happening in the world. The students are seated in groups of 3–4 students, who work individually to determine various strategies that can be used to solve a math problem posed by the teacher.

In addition to learning strategies for multiplication, the class has been working on showing perseverance as they work through problems in mathematics. The teacher has posted an "I can" statement on the board related to this ongoing goal: "I can persevere in solving a math problem using different strategies." Before beginning work on the problem, the teacher provides an opportunity for students to talk to a shoulder partner about the meaning of perseverance. The teacher then calls on several students in the class to define what it means to persevere before starting students on the task of the day.

The teacher posts the problem on the board. The problem is also recorded in the students' personal journals. When given the go-ahead by the teacher, students work individually to determine strategies that would help them solve the following problem:

> Mrs. Moore's class wants to go on a field trip. The class can earn money by running the school store. The students can earn $17 each week if they run the store. How much money can the class earn in 6 weeks?

The teacher monitors student learning during the lesson by circulating throughout the room and asking selected students to share their chosen strategies and the rationale for choosing them. Some students use pencil and paper, while others use manipulatives such as beans and cubes to help them solve the problem.

The teacher praises students for the strategies they have chosen, encourages them to be precise in their use of mathematical language, reminds them to show the steps in their work that reflect their thinking, and thanks them for their persistence in identifying strategies to solve the problem.

After time is provided for solving the problem, the teacher asks all students in the class to indicate with their fingers how many strategies they used to solve the problem. The number of strategies used by individual students ranges from three to six. During the course of the lesson, the teacher chooses two students to come up front to explain a math strategy that they chose to solve the problem, but the lesson ends before these explanations are delivered.

Step 2 - Preparation and Questions

- *Read the teacher's lesson plan and jot down things you expect to see and what you want to look for in the video of the lesson.*
- *Write down any questions or comments you have about the lesson plan.*

Step 3 – Viewing the Classroom Video

- *Watch the video of the entire lesson, noting those things you expected to see based on the lesson plan.*
- *Note what was missing based on your expectations from the lesson plan. Jot down significant behaviors of the teacher and students pertinent to the FFT Clusters.*
- *After watching the video, look at the samples of student work provided (if available).*

Step 4 – Selected Highlights of the Lesson Video

Read the highlights of the lesson provided below. Note those matching your highlights of the lesson. For each set of statements, determine the FFT Cluster that is best related to the behaviors presented.

A. The teacher posts the learning target, orally shares the learning target of the lesson, and makes sure that students understand what it means to "persevere" in the task assigned to them. (Cluster ___)

B. Teacher reviews expectations before starting students on independent work. The teacher asks, "What might I see you doing? What might I hear you saying?" (Cluster ___)

C. The problem that students are working on is posted on the board in front of the room for all to see. In addition, the students record the problem in their journals, and the teacher has students highlight/underline key words in the problem before students are asked to work on solving the problem independently. (Cluster ___)

D. The students are given a substantial amount of time to demonstrate their perseverance by working on one challenging problem. (6:37-39:00 minutes). (Cluster ___)

E. As the teacher circulates throughout the room, she asks students, "Tell me about your thinking. Tell me about why you chose this strategy?" (Cluster ___)

F. The teacher provides time for students to explain their thinking without interrupting the students' explanations. (Cluster ___)

G. The teacher specifically praises students who, through their writing or illustration, show their thinking of how they solved the problem. The teacher also insists that students use precise mathematical language. (Cluster ___)

H. The teacher provides manipulatives for students who need them to solve the problem. The retrieval of these materials occurs with little disruption and little loss of instructional time.

(Cluster ____)

Step 5 – Viewing the Teacher Commentary

Watch the video of the teacher's commentary about the lesson and jot down any questions or comments you have about the commentary. Read the highlights below and identify the related FFT Cluster.

A. The teacher explains that she has focused on building conceptual understanding of multiplication and developing fluency in multiplication. This lesson allows students to apply their learning by solving a real world mathematics problem. The teacher explains that the students will continue to solve real world problems in mathematics so that they can make the connections between what they are learning in school and what is happening in the real world. The current lesson will be extended when students are asked to write in the Math Center about their favorite strategy for solving the problem and to justify their answers. (Cluster ____)

B. The teacher also emphasizes that the class has been focusing on perseverance in solving problems. Students have focused on solving problems in different ways and also coaching their peers when they don't understand. She has sought to create a safe environment for risk taking by teaching students Accountable Talk stems that help students agree, disagree, and provide feedback to each other in non-threatening ways. (Cluster ____)

Step 6 – Questions, Applications, and Discussion

The purpose of this step is to prompt your analysis and reflection of the Instructional Set and to have you think about applications to your own practice.

1. **Teaching and Learning Related to the FFT Clusters**

The purpose of the activity is to increase your understanding of the relationship between the highlights of the Instructional Set and the FFT Clusters. Your identification of an FFT Cluster for each of the highlights is compared to the Cluster identified by the master coders. The Answer Key is located at the end of the activities. You have options on how to complete the comparison. Determine what might work best for your group's learning. Options include, but are not limited to the following.

- Look at the first set of highlights. Take a poll of what each group member identified as the related FFT Cluster. If all members said the same FFT Cluster, have one or two

members say why. Compare the group's response to the answer sheet. Repeat for the remainder of the highlights.

OR

- Have each member take one or two highlights. State the correct answer for each one, and a reason why the highlight demonstrates that FFT Cluster. The member will facilitate a discussion if others had different responses, with the goal of having all understand the justification of the correct answer.

OR

- Have members check their own responses to all the highlights. If there are any incorrect answers, then the member selects one highlight and leads a discussion with the group to learn why others think the highlight matches the correct FFT Cluster.

OR

- Determine your own process to check and discuss the match between highlights and the FFT Clusters.

2. **Analysis and Reflection of the Instructional Set**

The purpose of this activity for you to analyze and reflect on what you saw and heard in the artifacts and videos, to share your analysis with your peers, and to discuss some of the questions or comments you noted. Review the notes, comments, and questions you recorded when you examined the Instructional Set.

a. Identify a key teaching and learning attribute demonstrated in the Instructional Set that was effective and state why you think it worked well.

b. Identify a different attribute that could be enhanced or improved, and provide ideas about how it could be improved.

c. Share your statements with your group and have your peers react to and build upon your analysis and ideas.

Sample statements:

The students in this class seem familiar with behavioral expectations and, for the most part, are able to work on the problem for a long period of time without asking for the teacher's or their peer's assistance. This is effective because many teachers struggle with establishing and maintaining clear expectations for student behavior when students are not being directly supervised by the teacher. There are instances, however, when students get up from their seats and approach the teacher for assistance. The teacher tells at least two students to go back to their seats while she is working with another student. When two other students leave their seats and come up to the teacher, she immediately provides an answer that meets their needs. In one case, she goes to that student's desk to provide assistance. Some students might see this as showing favoritism. The teacher's actions are less effective in these instances, since they appear to go against the established expectations for the class. I wonder if the teacher could have selected students beforehand that other students could approach for assistance before coming to her, to allow for more student assumption of responsibility. Some teachers use the "ask three before me" method. Might that method work for these students?

Additional ideas for statements:

- Monitor the pacing of the lesson to allow for whole group sharing before the lesson ends.
- Differentiate problems to allow for student choice and/ or greater degrees of difficulty for students who can meet the challenge.
- Create opportunities for students to share their thinking with partners and/or coach each other.

3. **Notice, Learn, and Apply**

The purpose of this activity is for you to reflect on what you learned from your analysis of the Instructional Set, and to determine how you will apply it to your teaching.

- Complete the statements:
  "I noticed _____ ."
  (Insert one thing you noticed about the teacher or students.)

  "And I learned _____ ."
  (State what you learned related to what you noticed.)

  "I will apply what I learned by _____ ."
  (Provide example of how you will use what you learned in your own context.)
- Share your statements with your group. Have others react and also add how they might apply what you noticed to their own teaching context.

Sample statements:

- I noticed that the students were able to persevere in finding multiple strategies for the same problem.
- I learned that when students are given enough time and supports, they can demonstrate their ability to think about the same problem in various ways and can recall many strategies that they have been taught over the course of a unit. I usually give students multiple problems and ask them to demonstrate two ways to solve each problem.
- I will apply what I learned by allowing students more time to think deeply about one problem, provide manipulatives to solve problems if necessary, and use this as a way to build student stamina and perseverance.

Study Guide for Teachers Answer Key

Highlights from the
Lesson Video
(Step 4)

A. The teacher posts the learning target, orally shares the learning target of the lesson, and makes sure that students understand what it means to "persevere" in the task assigned to them. (Cluster 4 Student Intellectual Engagement)

B. Teacher reviews expectations before starting students on independent work. The teacher asks, "What might I see you doing? What might I hear you saying?" (Cluster 2 Safe, Respectful, Supportive, and Challenging Learning Environment)

C. The problem that students are working on is posted on the board in front of the room for all to see. In addition, the students record the problem in their journals, and the teacher has students highlight/underline key words in the problem before students are asked to work on solving the problem independently. (Cluster 3 Classroom Management)

D. The students are given a substantial amount of time to demonstrate their perseverance by working on one challenging problem. (6:37-39:00 minutes). (Cluster 4 Student Intellectual Engagement)

E. As the teacher circulates throughout the room, she asks students, "Tell me about your thinking. Tell me about why you chose this strategy." (Cluster 4 Student Intellectual Engagement)

F. The teacher provides time for students to explain their thinking without interrupting the students' explanations. (Cluster 5 Successful Learning for All Students)

G. The teacher specifically praises students who, through their writing or illustration, show their thinking of how they solved the problem. The teacher also insists that students use precise mathematical language. (Cluster 4 Student Intellectual Engagement)

H. The teacher provides manipulatives for students who need them to solve the problem. The retrieval of these materials occurs with little disruption and little loss of instructional time. (Cluster 3 Classroom Management)

Study Guide for Teachers Answer Key

Highlights from the
Teacher Commentary
(Step 5)

A. The teacher explains that she has focused on building conceptual understanding of multiplication and developing fluency in multiplication. This lesson allows students to apply their learning by solving a real world mathematics problem. The teacher explains that the students will continue to solve real world problems in mathematics so that they can make the connections between what they are learning in school and what is happening in the real world. The current lesson will be extended when students are asked to write in the Math Center about their favorite strategy for solving the problem and to justify their answers. (Cluster 1 Clarity of Instructional Purpose and Accuracy of Content)

B. The teacher also emphasizes that the class has been focusing on perseverance in solving problems. Students have focused on solving problems in different ways and also coaching their peers when they don't understand. She has sought to create a safe environment for risk taking by teaching students Accountable Talk stems that help students agree, disagree, and provide feedback to each other in non-threatening ways. (Cluster 5 Successful Learning by All Students)

FFT Clusters Study Guide: Set 1 (Math 3)

**Looking at Teaching Through
the Lens of the FFT Clusters**

A Study Guide for
Instructional Coach
Learning Communities

Teacher: Penney
Subject: Mathematics
Grade: 3
Topic: Perseverance, Solving
Using Different Strategies

Welcome to the Study Guide for the Penney Math Instructional Set, a collection of artifacts and videos for an instructional lesson. This Study Guide provides information and instructions on how to examine teaching and learning through the lens of the Framework for Teaching (FFT) Clusters. In order to complete the steps in this Guide, you will need access to the teacher's planning documents, the lesson video, and the teacher commentary video (http://www.danielsongroup.org/study-guides/). This Study Guide has been designed so Steps 1–5 focus on examining the Instructional Set and can be done by an individual. Step 6 is a group activity and focuses on proposed interactions with the featured teacher and applications of learning.

Step 1 - Lesson Overview

Read the background information of the lesson provided below.

This lesson is an application of what students have been learning about multiplication. The teacher states that she uses real-world problems to help students make connections from the math they are learning in school to what is happening in the world. The students are seated in groups of 3–4 students, who work individually to determine various strategies that can be used to solve a math problem posed by the teacher.

In addition to learning strategies for multiplication, the class has been working on showing perseverance as they work through problems in mathematics. The teacher has posted an "I can" statement on the board related to this ongoing goal: "I can persevere in solving a math problem using different strategies." Before beginning work on the problem, the teacher provides an opportunity for students to talk to a shoulder partner about the meaning of perseverance. The teacher then calls on several students in the class to define what it means to persevere before starting students on the task of the day.

The teacher posts the problem on the board. The problem is also recorded in the students' personal journals. When given the go-ahead by the teacher, students work individually to determine strategies that would help them solve the following problem:

> Mrs. Moore's class wants to go on a field trip. The class can earn money by running the school store. The students can earn $17 each week if they run the store. How much money can the class earn in 6 weeks?

The teacher monitors student learning during the lesson by circulating throughout the room and asking selected students to share their chosen strategies and the rationale for choosing them. Some students use pencil and paper, while others use manipulatives such as beans and cubes to help them solve the problem.

The teacher praises students for the strategies they have chosen, encourages them to be precise in their use of mathematical language, reminds them to show the steps in their work that reflect their thinking, and thanks them for their persistence in identifying strategies to solve the problem.

After time is provided for solving the problem, the teacher asks all students in the class to indicate with their fingers how many strategies they used to solve the problem. The number of strategies used by individual students ranges from three to six. During the course of the lesson, the teacher chooses two students to come up front to explain a math strategy that they chose to solve the problem, but the lesson ends before these explanations are delivered.

Step 2 - Preparation and Questions

- *Read the teacher's lesson plan and jot down things you expect to see and what you want to look for in the video of the lesson.*
- *Write down any questions or comments you have about the lesson plan.*

Step 3 – Viewing the Classroom Video

- *Watch the video of the entire lesson, noting those things you expected to see based on the lesson plan.*
- *Note what was missing based on your expectations from the lesson plan. Jot down significant behaviors of the teacher and students pertinent to the FFT Clusters.*
- *After watching the video, look at the samples of student work provided (if available).*

Step 4 – Selected Highlights of the Lesson Video

Read the highlights of the lesson provided below. Note those matching your highlights of the lesson. For each set of statements, determine the FFT Cluster that is best related to the behaviors presented.

A. The teacher posts the learning target, orally shares the learning target of the lesson, and makes sure that students understand what it means to "persevere" in the task assigned to them. (Cluster ___)

B. Teacher reviews expectations before starting students on independent work. The teacher asks, "What might I see you doing? What might I hear you saying?" (Cluster ___)

C. The problem that students are working on is posted on the board in front of the room for all to see. In addition, the students record the problem in their journals, and the teacher has students highlight/ underline key words in the problem before students are asked to work on solving the problem independently. (Cluster ___)

D. The students are given a substantial amount of time to demonstrate their perseverance by working on one challenging problem. (6:37-39:00 minutes). (Cluster ___)

E. As the teacher circulates throughout the room, she asks students, "Tell me about your thinking. Tell me about why you chose this strategy?" (Cluster ___)

F. The teacher provides time for students to explain their thinking without interrupting the students' explanations. (Cluster ___)

G. The teacher specifically praises students who, through their writing or illustration, show their thinking of how they solved the problem. The teacher also insists that students use precise mathematical language. (Cluster ___)

H. The teacher provides manipulatives for students who need them to solve the problem. The retrieval of these materials occurs with little disruption and little loss of instructional time.

(Cluster ___)

Step 5 – Viewing the Teacher Commentary

Watch the video of the teacher's commentary about the lesson and jot down any questions or comments you have about the commentary. Read the highlights below and identify the related FFT Cluster.

A. The teacher explains that she has focused on building conceptual understanding of multiplication and developing fluency in multiplication. This lesson allows students to apply their learning by solving a real world mathematics problem. The teacher explains that the students will continue to solve real world problems in mathematics so that they can make the connections between what they are learning in school and what is happening in the real world. The current lesson will be extended when students are asked to write in the Math Center about their favorite strategy for solving the problem and to justify their answers. (Cluster ___)

B. The teacher also emphasizes that the class has been focusing on perseverance in solving problems. Students have focused on solving problems in different ways and also coaching their peers when they don't understand. She has sought to create a safe environment for risk taking by teaching students Accountable Talk stems that help students agree, disagree, and provide feedback to each other in non-threatening ways. (Cluster ___)

Step 6 – Questions, Applications, and Discussion

The purpose of this step is to prompt your analysis of and reflection on the Instructional Set and to have you think about applications to your own practice.

1. **Preparation for professional conversation with the featured teacher**

The purpose of the activity is to increase your understanding of the relationship between the highlights of the Instructional Set and the FFT Clusters. Your identification of an FFT Cluster for each of the highlights is compared to the Cluster identified by the master coders. The Answer Key is located at the end of the activities. You have options on how to complete the comparison. Determine what might work best for your group's learning. Options include, but are not limited to the following.

- Look at the first set of highlights. Take a poll of what each group member identified as the related FFT Cluster. If all members said the same FFT Cluster, have one or two

members say why. Compare the group's response to the answer sheet. Repeat for the remainder of the highlights.

OR

- Have each member take one or two highlights. State the correct answer for each one, and a reason why the highlight demonstrates that FFT Cluster. The member will facilitate a discussion if others had different responses, with the goal of having all understand the justification of the correct answer.

OR

- Have members check their own responses to all the highlights. If there are any incorrect answers, then the member selects one highlight and leads a discussion with the group to learn why others think the highlight matches the correct FFT Cluster.

OR

- Determine your own process to check and discuss the match between highlights and the FFT Clusters.

2. **Analysis and Reflection of the Instructional Set**
The purpose of this activity for you to analyze and reflect on what you saw and heard in the artifacts and videos and discuss some of the questions or comments you noted.

This activity provides you and your peers the opportunity to practice preparing questions to get more information about the teacher's thinking and the behaviors of both students and the teacher, which is one element of a professional conversation. The feedback from your peers about your questions should include to what extent they are appropriate and will obtain useful information without making the featured teacher feel uneasy or criticized. The second part of this activity focuses on helping teachers move their practice forward. Please note that having you prepare for and model an entire conversation about the lesson with the featured teacher is not the purpose of this activity as written. Your group can modify or replace the activity to meet your group's needs.

a. Review the notes, comments, and questions you recorded when you examined the Instructional Set. Pretend you have the opportunity to ask the teacher some questions to get additional information about the strategies used or decisions made for this Instructional Set.

b. Next, think of what you would say to prompt the teacher's thinking about how to enhance their practice. Share with your group just the questions you would use with the teacher to elicit additional information. Have your peers comment about your questions and add other questions they had about the same event.

c. Share with others in your group what you would do to prompt the teacher's thinking and actions to enhance his/her practice. Take turns sharing and discussing the prompts.

Sample A:

Part 1 – I noticed that during the lesson, you collected notes as you spoke one-on-one with selected students. What types of notes do you collect based upon the task that the students are completing? Can you share some of the strategies you use to assess student learning during the course of instruction?

Part 2 – One important aspect of student assessment is self-assessment. What are some of the strategies that you might use to allow students to assess their own learning? Are there some strategies that you can incorporate so that students can assess their progress over time, or that can challenge them to continue to move forward in their thinking? What benefits might you and your students reap if you have students track the amount of time they are able to persevere on a given problem or if they have improved on the number of strategies that they use to solve problems?

Sample B:

Part 1 – You asked two students if they would be willing to share their strategies with the class. Unfortunately, we did not get to see this during the time that we observed the lesson. Students were not observed speaking to their peers at their tables about the strategies that they used. Tell me a little more about how you selected the students that would share their strategies? In what instances is it preferable to wait until the end to have selected students share their strategies, as opposed to having students do so during the time that they are working on the problems? When might you do both?

Part 2 – As you circulated the room, I noticed that you stopped at the desks of selected students and asked them to explain their strategies and the rationale for the selection of those strategies. Even at the same table, students used different strategies and were comfortable getting manipulatives if that helped them to demonstrate the use of a different strategy. Most students were able to explain their strategies and their thinking as they worked through the problem.

Two girls in particular had difficulty explaining their thinking. For one of the girls, you acknowledged that sometimes it is hard to explain your thinking to others. For the other girl, you told her that you would come back to her but you did not come back to her by the end of the lesson. What methods have you tried to help students to become better at articulating their thinking? Perhaps you can try having a student listen to a student who used the same strategy and then articulate their thinking in their own words. How do you think that might work with your students?

3. **Notice, Learn and Apply**

The purpose of this activity is for you to reflect on what you learned from your analysis of the Instructional Set, and to determine how you will apply it to your coaching.

- Complete the statements:
  "I noticed _____."
  (Insert one thing you noticed about the teacher or students.)

  "And I learned _____."
  (State what you learned related to what you noticed.)

  "I will apply what I learned by _____."
  (Provide example of how you will use what you learned in your own context.)

- Share your statements with your group and have others react and add how they might apply what you noticed to their own coaching context.

Sample statements:

- I noticed how challenging it can be for some students to explain their thinking.
- I learned that some students will need support to help them get better at articulating their thinking.
- I will apply what I learned by using the video to identify strategies that the teacher used to encourage meta-cognition. I will also research additional strategies that can be used to get students to "think about their thinking" and become more proficient at explaining it, perhaps using questioning prompts.

Study Guide for Instructional Coaches Answer Key

Highlights from the
Lesson Video
(Step 4)

A. The teacher posts the learning target, orally shares the learning target of the lesson, and makes sure that students understand what it means to "persevere" in the task assigned to them. (Cluster 4 Student Intellectual Engagement)

B. Teacher reviews expectations before starting students on independent work. The teacher asks, "What might I see you doing? What might I hear you saying?" (Cluster 2 Safe, Respectful, Supportive, and Challenging Learning Environment)

C. The problem that students are working on is posted on the board in front of the room for all to see. In addition, the students record the problem in their journals, and the teacher has students highlight/underline key words in the problem before students are asked to work on solving the problem independently. (Cluster 3 Classroom Management)

D. The students are given a substantial amount of time to demonstrate their perseverance by working on one challenging problem. (6:37-39:00 minutes). (Cluster 4 Student Intellectual Engagement)

E. As the teacher circulates throughout the room, she asks students, "Tell me about your thinking. Tell me about why you chose this strategy." (Cluster 4 Student Intellectual Engagement)

F. The teacher provides time for students to explain their thinking without interrupting the students' explanations. (Cluster 5 Successful Learning for All Students)

G. The teacher specifically praises students who, through their writing or illustration, show their thinking of how they solved the problem. The teacher also insists that students use precise mathematical language. (Cluster 4 Student Intellectual Engagement)

H. The teacher provides manipulatives for students who need them to solve the problem. The retrieval of these materials occurs with little disruption and little loss of instructional time. (Cluster 3 Classroom Management)

Study Guide for Instructional Coaches Answer Key

A. The teacher explains that she has focused on building conceptual understanding of multiplication and developing fluency in multiplication. This lesson allows students to apply their learning by solving a real world mathematics problem. The teacher explains that the students will continue to solve real world problems in mathematics so that they can make the connections between what they are learning in school and what is happening in the real world. The current lesson will be extended when students are asked to write in the Math Center about their favorite strategy for solving the problem and to justify their answers. (Cluster 1 Clarity of Instructional Purpose and Accuracy of Content)

B. The teacher also emphasizes that the class has been focusing on perseverance in solving problems. Students have focused on solving problems in different ways and also coaching their peers when they don't understand. She has sought to create a safe environment for risk taking by teaching students Accountable Talk stems that help students agree, disagree, and provide feedback to each other in non-threatening ways. (Cluster 5 Successful Learning by All Students)

Record of Evidence

This Record of Evidence (ROE) contains key evidence aligned to the FFT Clusters. Interpretive statements about the evidence are also provided. The ROE was created by two master coders who recorded evidence and interpretation statements independently, reviewed each others' work, and arrived at a final composite version based on their professional conversations. This version was reviewed by a leader of the master coders. The ROE is included in this Study Guide so users can see what master coders identified as key evidence, and their interpretation of that evidence through the lens of the FFT Clusters. It is provided as an example of one type of analysis of an Instructional Set. The ROEs were created for professional development rather than evaluative purposes. Users are cautioned about using them for teacher evaluation.

Rubric:	Generic
Grade:	3
Subject:	Math
Topic:	Perseverance, Solving Using Different Strategies
Teacher description:	Female, caucasian, experience unknown
Class description:	23 students (13 boys/10 girls) 8% SPED, 13% RTI, 0% Gifted and Talented 79% Caucasian, 4% Hispanic, 4% Asian, and 13% Multiracial
Artifacts:	• Instructional Plan • Teacher Commentary • Student Work Samples
Length of video:	39:50

Cluster 1:   Clarity of Instructional Purpose and Accuracy of Content

Guiding Questions

- *To what extent does the teacher demonstrate depth of important content knowledge and conduct the class with a clear and ambitious purpose, reflective of the standards for the discipline and appropriate to the students' levels of knowledge and skill?*

- *To what degree are the elements of a lesson (the sequence of topics, instructional strategies, and materials and resources) well designed and executed, and aligned with the purpose of the lesson?*

- *To what extent are they designed to engage students in high-level learning in the discipline?*

Record of Evidence

Evidence

Instructional Plan

- The teacher's lesson plan is correlated to the following standards regarding representing and solving problems involving multiplication and division: CCSS Math Standard: 3.OA.A.3 Represent and solve problems involving multiplication and division: Use multiplication and division within 100 to solve word problems in situations involving equal groups, arrays, and measurement quantities, e.g., by using drawings and equations with a symbol for the unknown number to represent the problem.
- Aspects of rigor called for by the standard being addressed in this lesson:
  - Application – primary
  - Conceptual Understanding – secondary
- The teacher notes the materials students will be using:
  - Spiral Notebooks
  - Math tools: Base Ten blocks, counters, etc.
  - Story problem for Student Math Journals
- The lesson plan includes the following learning goals and student objectives:
  Learning Goals:
  - To persevere in solving math problem involving finding equal groups
  - To use drawings, equations, and/or math tools to solve math problems that involve finding equal groups
  - To use precise mathematical vocabulary such as factors, product, and array while justifying answers in math solutions
  - To justify answers in math solutions
  Student Objectives:
  - To identify as many different combinations as possible using a method of choice to assist a student in solving the problem (e.g., arrays, counters, pictures, etc.)
  - To use drawing, equations, and/or math tools to solve math problems that involve equal groups
  - To engage in a partner, small group, and whole class discussion explaining and justifying students' math thinking
- The students will solve this problem:
  Mrs. Moore's class wants to go on a field trip. The class can earn money by running the school store. The students can earn $17 each week if they run the store. How much money can the class earn in 6 weeks?
  - The teacher will begin the lesson discussing the learning goals with the students (goals will be written on the board) and telling students they will record their thinking and reasoning in their Math Journals.
  - The teacher will pose the problem to the class; it is also in their Math Journal. The teacher will monitor the students' thinking and problem-solving by asking students to explain their thinking.
  - The teacher will be looking for: the math tool used for solving (student choice), perseverance to find all the different combinations to solve the problem, thinking and reasoning.

Record of Evidence

Cluster 1: Clarity of Instructional Purpose and Accuracy of Content

Evidence (cont'd.)

- – The teacher will invite students to present their solutions and/or strategies. Students will participate in whole class discussion to ask questions for clarification, understanding, and/or extensions to a solution/strategy.
- – The teacher will present patterns to solutions and discuss with class. She will look for levels in problem representation and solutions (as stated in the Progression Documents):
  1. Level 1: Making and counting all quantities in multiplication and division with objects or a diagram. Student uses either the objects or diagram to explain thinking. This would include arrays and counting of objects.
  2. Level 2: Repeated counting by a given number, such as 6, 12, 18, 24, etc. (e.g., student counts by sixes and tracks how many sixes are used).
  3. Level 3: Use of the associative or distributive property to compose and decompose numbers in finding a solution. For example: 6 x 17= (6 x 10) + (6 x 7). Students may decompose a product they do not know to one that they do know and then build from there.
- The teacher has designed questions as a review of the learning goal:
  - – Ask: What was the first step you took in solving this problem of finding equal groups? Action: Have student partner share and then call on one/two students to share.
  - – Ask: Give an example of how you persevered when finding as many equal groups possible? Action: Students will share with a partner and one/two will share with whole class.
  - – Ask: What helped you persevere? Action: Select a few students to share.
  - – Ask: Describe one or two things you learned from another person's justification. Action: Have students share with a partner and ask a few students to share with whole class.
  - – Ask: Was a solution or strategy presented today that you had not thought about using that you might use the next time you will find equal groups? Action: Have those students share their thinking.
- The teacher will highlight a few moments from the lesson that she observed students either persevering or using a solution/strategy.
- In closing, the teacher will say, "We will continue to find equal groups in real world problems, and I encourage you to build upon your knowledge from your work today to help you with future problems."

Interview
- The teacher states, "I have built on conceptual understanding of multiplication so they can have an understanding of what multiplication is. We started with conceptual and then we go to fluency. This is an example of an application lesson for multiplication."

Record of Evidence

Cluster 1: Clarity of Instructional Purpose and Accuracy of Content

Evidence (cont'd.)

- "We have worked on a safe environment, number talks, solving problems in different ways, persevering… and have done a lot of coaching when someone doesn't understand or disagrees. They agree and disagree and build on each other's answers. Re-voicing so others' can access their thinking. After the lesson, students will choose one of their favorite or most effective strategies and write about it at the Math Center to justify their answers. They will continue to solve real world multiplication problems so they see that connection."

Video
- There are several math charts on the walls.
- The teacher introduces the lesson and tells the students what they will be doing. She asks students what perseverance means; students talk in their groups.
- T: Boys and Girls, we have been working on persevering and solving math problems. Today we are going to persevere in solving math problems using different strategies.
- Students share what it means to persevere.
- T: When you are working on your problem today, what might I see you doing and what might I hear you saying?
- Students talk to partners and share answers with large group.
- The teacher tells the students to find the problem in their Math Journal and read it silently.
- Teacher reads problem from the white board. T: What information is important? Emma?
- S: $17 each week and 6 weeks. (Teacher underlines on white board.)
- T: Mrs. Moore and field trip. Perfect.
- The teacher reads the problem from the white board and students identify what is important.
- The teacher tells the students to solve this problem using different strategies.
- T: Tell me why you are using this strategy.
- T: Why did you choose this number?
- T: Is this a reasonable answer?
- T: How is this helping you solve the problem?
- T: Alright, thank you for labeling your answer.
- T: Thanks for using precision and labeling correctly.
- T: Thanks for being precise.

Record of Evidence

Cluster 1:   **Clarity of Instructional Purpose and Accuracy of Content**

Interpretation
- The teacher is clear in stating the instructional purpose and correlation with the CCSS appropriate for the students' levels of knowledge and skill.
- The teacher demonstrates a depth of content knowledge during the interview and conducts the class with a clear purpose.
- The teacher designs several questions that are aligned to the instructional purpose.
- The materials, strategies, and activities are appropriate and aligned with the instructional outcome. The elements of the lesson are designed to engage students in high-level learning.
- There is no evidence of differentiation.
- Students demonstrate higher-level learning through application and analysis of multiple methods to find solutions to a problem.

Record of Evidence

Cluster 2: Safe, Respectful, Supportive, and Challenging Learning Environment

Guiding Questions

- *To what extent do the interactions between teacher and students, and among students, demonstrate genuine caring and a safe, respectful, supportive, and also challenging learning environment?*

- *Do teachers convey high expectations for student learning and encourage hard work and perseverance? Is the environment safe for risk taking?*

- *Do students take pride in their work and demonstrate a commitment to mastering challenging content?*

Evidence
- A quote is displayed on the white board about perseverance, "I can persevere…."
- The teacher calls the students by first name.
- The lesson begins with the teacher asking students what perseverance means.
- S: Keep trying and never give up?
- S: Make a plan and if that doesn't work, make a new plan.
- The teacher tells the students to find the problem in their Math Journal and read it silently.
- T: I like the way I see people highlighting important information.
- S: How many students are there?
- T: I don't think it matters. Is that important information? Okay, I will talk with you about that in a second.
- T: Thanks for showing your work so I can see how you are solving that problem.
- Student walks to teacher and shows his work. T: Okay, have a seat and I will talk with you in a second.
- The teacher kneels by several students when she monitors their work.
- T: (kneels by student) Tell me your thinking on this. S: (inaudible) T: Okay. Let's check it; count with me. Teacher continues to work with this student until she is able to verbalize it. T: So you did the problem correct but you had a hard time verbalizing it. You did okay, that's fantastic. Sometimes it is hard to explain your thinking, but that's okay. Fantastic. Correct.
- T: Thank you for persevering. Would you mind sharing this answer when it's time to share? S: Sure.
- Student in gray sweatshirt talks to teacher. T (puts hand on his shoulder): Okay.
- All students are on task all of the time, indicating that their activity is cognitively challenging.

Record of Evidence

Cluster 2: **Safe, Respectful, Supportive, and Challenging Learning Environment**

Interpretation
- Interactions between the teacher and the students and among the students are uniformly respectful.
- There are high levels of cognitive energy.
- The students persevere during the lesson with very few questions for the teacher. Students share their work willingly with the teacher.
- The teacher has high expectations for students' capabilities for learning. She works with each student until they understand.
- Two students are willing to share their work in front of classmates.
- Students immediately engage in small group discussions and problem solving work.

Record of Evidence

Cluster 3:   Classroom Management

Guiding Questions

- *Is the classroom well run and organized?*

- *Are classroom routines and procedures clear and carried out efficiently by both teacher and students with little loss of instructional time?*

- *To what extent do students themselves take an active role in their smooth operation?*

- *Are directions for activities clearly explained so that there is no confusion?*

- *Do students not only understand and comply with standards of conduct, but also play an active part in setting the tone for maintaining those standards?*

- *How does the physical environment support the learning activities?*

Evidence

- The students are sitting in groups of three and four, and have access to the board.
- T: What does perseverance mean? Talk in your groups. Students immediately talk in small groups.
- T: 5, 4, 3, 2, 1 (to bring their attention back to her). Students immediately are quiet.
- T: Turn to your neighbor and share. Students talk to neighbor.
- T: 3, 2, 1 (students are quiet).
- T: Who can repeat what Hunter said, in his words or your words?
- T: What might I see you doing and what might I hear you saying? Very quickly. Shoulder partners. Students talk to partners. Teacher walks from group to group.
- T: 5, 4, 3, 2, 1 (students quit talking immediately).
- Teacher repeats the questions.
- T: 3, 2…(students are quiet.)
- The teacher tells the students to find the problem in their Math Journal and read it silently.
- T: I like the way I see people highlighting important information. (The teacher did not tell the students to highlight.)
- T: Please. Sit quietly, please, while others have a chance to read it. The teacher takes a paper away from a student and he retrieves one of them.
- Some students who are finished with their problems play with manipulatives, and do not interfere or talk with other students.
- T: Boys and girls, fist to 5, how much time do you need? (Students respond.) Okay, I will give you about 5 more minutes. Thank you for persevering and solving this problem in different ways.
- Show me with hand signals, how many different ways you used to solve the problem.

Record of Evidence

Cluster 3: **Classroom Management**

Interpretation
- The classroom is well run and organized. There are behavior expectations on a chart hanging in the classroom. Students do not need to move from one group to another and have all of their materials. There is no loss of instructional time.
- All students are productively engaged during small group work.
- Teacher has a respectful approach to students. Her tone is gentle, and she listens carefully when students speak to her.
- The teacher's monitoring of student behavior is seamless and preventative. Student behavior is appropriate.
- The physical environment supports the learning activities.

Record of Evidence

Cluster 4:   Student Intellectual Engagement

Guiding Questions

- *To what extent are students intellectually engaged in a classroom of high intellectual energy?*

- *What is the nature of what students are doing?*

- *Are they being challenged to think and make connections through both the instructional activities and the questions explored?*

- *Do the teacher's explanations of content correctly model academic language and invite intellectual work by students?*

- *Are students asked to explain their thinking, to construct logical arguments citing evidence, and to question the thinking of others?*

- *Are the instructional strategies used by the teacher suitable to the discipline, and to what extent do they promote student agency in the learning of challenging content?*

Evidence

- The lesson begins with a review. Students talk in small groups and share with the class.
- T: Who would like to share what it means to persevere?
- S: Use tools and strategies.
- S: Keep trying and never give up.
- T: Anyone want to add on to that?
- S: If your answer is way off, you can do ball park estimates.
- S: Make a plan and if that doesn't work, make a another plan.
- T: Turn to your neighbor and share.
- T: Who can repeat what Hunter said in his words or your words?
- S: Change your plans.
- T: When you are working on your problem today, what might I see you doing and what might I hear you saying? Very quickly, shoulder partners.
- Students talk to partners.
- Teacher walks from group to group.
- Teacher repeats the questions and students answer.
- T: Math vocabulary. Choose someone to add on or share something different.
- Students use Accountable Talk and other sentence starters.
- S: Coaching…help out others if they are stuck…choose one more person, lucky last.
- T: Find the problem in your Math Journal and read it silently.
- T: Solve this problem using different strategies. Ready begin.

Record of Evidence

Cluster 4:   Student Intellectual Engagement

Evidence (cont'd.)

- Students work individually and quietly. All students are engaged.
- The teacher moves from student to student, asking questions to challenge thinking and make connections. The teacher asks the students to cite evidence.
- T to S: Tell me why you are using this strategy. Student responds. T: Tell about the numbers you chose. S: (inaudible) T: Fantastic, great job.
- Teacher is using a clipboard and recording.
- T to S: Tell me your thinking. Why did you choose this number? S: (inaudible)
- The teacher gets on her knees by student and asks student to show her how she solved the problem. Student answers. T: Tell me your thinking. Tell me why you connected some of these circles. Tell me what you did with these. Is that a reasonable answer, does it make sense? S: Uh huh.
- T: Tell me why….that's part of persevering right? If you make a plan and it doesn't work, you make another plan.
- T: Would you tell me why you used this strategy?
- T: Tell me why you chose this strategy. Student responds. Teacher asks more questions and student responds.
- T: Can you tell me your thinking on this? S: (inaudible).
- T: How many Xs are here? S: 17.
- T: Tell me what you did here? S: (inaudible).
- T: How many groups of 17 do you have? S: 6.
- T: Why are there 6? S: (inaudible).
- T: What are these numbers on the side? S: (inaudible). Student thinks and explains.
- T: Go ahead and check your answer and then you may want to rethink something here.
- The teacher works with all students, and with three students three different times.
- T (to student in pink shirt): How did you figure out how many Xs there were in that array? Tell me how you solved it. What could you write on your paper so I could see how you are solving it?
- T: Is this an efficient strategy, a strategy you are comfortable with using, a strategy that you know you can get the answer? Student works on problem.
- T: I will come back when you have your strategy. Student thinks for a while and then starts working.
- The teacher wraps up the lesson at 39:27.
- T: Okay, boys and girls, our time for solving the problem is up. Show me with hand signals, how many different ways you used to solve the problem. How many strategies? Students respond. T: I see 5, 6, 3, excellent job, 9.

Record of Evidence

Cluster 4: Student Intellectual Engagement

Interpretation
- The teacher provides a review activity at the beginning of the lesson.
- The teacher leads the students in a large group discussion about what is important in the problem.
- The students work on the problem using a choice of strategies.
- All students are intellectually engaged in the problem-solving and are able to explain their thinking and why they used the strategies they chose.

Record of Evidence

Cluster 5: **Successful Learning by All Students**

Guiding Questions

- *To what extent does the teacher ensure learning by all students?*

- *Does the teacher monitor student understanding through specifically designed questions or instructional techniques?*

- *To what extent do students monitor their own learning and provide respectful feedback to classmates?*

- *Does the teacher make modifications in presentations or learning activities where necessary, taking into account the degree of student learning?*

- *Has he or she sought out other resources (including parents) to support students' learning?*

- *In reflection, is the teacher aware of the success of the lesson in reaching students?*

Evidence

- The teacher monitors student learning by talking with each student and asking them to explain how they used the strategy/ies and how they got their answers. She records levels of student in problem representation and solution (as stated in the Progression Document).
- The teacher tells the students to solve the problem using different strategies.
- T: Tell me your thinking. Why did you choose this number? S: (inaudible). Teacher records on clipboard.
- Teacher asks student to show her how she solved the problem. S: (inaudible). T: Tell me your thinking. S: (inaudible). Tell me why you connected some of these circles. S: (inaudible). T: Tell me what you did with these. S: (inaudible). T: Is that a reasonable answer, does it make sense? S: Uh huh.
- T: Would you tell me why you used this strategy?
- T: Tell me why you chose this strategy. Student responds. Teacher asks more questions and student responds.
- Teacher looks at several students' work records on clipboard.
- T: Can you tell me your thinking on this? S: (inaudible).
- T: How many Xs are here? S: 17.
- T: Tell me what you did here? S: (inaudible).
- T: How many groups of 17 do you have? S: 6.
- T: Why are there 6? S: (inaudible).
- T: What are these numbers on the side? S: (inaudible). Student thinks and explains. T: Go ahead and check your answer and then you may want to rethink something here.
- T: Tell me why you chose this one. Student responds. T: Okay

Record of Evidence

Cluster 5:   Successful Learning by All Students

Evidence (cont'd.)

- T: Why did you choose this strategy to solve the problem? Student responds.
- T: How is this helping you to solve this problem? Student responds.
- Student is using manipulatives to work out the problem.
- T: Interesting, tell me how you solved this one. Student responds. T: so your answer is? S: 102 dollars. T: Can you be precise and (inaudible) that for me, please?
- T: Tell me again how you are using these math tools to solve your problem. Student responds. T: How are you going to get your answer? Student responds. T: Then what are you going to do? Student responds. T: So, it's just a different way to solve this problem. Is this a reasonable answer? How do you know? How do you know this is correct? Student responds, explaining the calculations. T: All right, thank you for labeling your answer.
- T (reflection from the commentary): Students were sharing multiple strategies, discussing and responding to each other's strategies so they can deepen their understanding of multiplication so they could have a tool belt of strategies.

Interpretation
- The teacher talks to students individually to monitor their learning. She asks specific questions.
- The teacher monitors the summative assessment for the learning outcomes.
- The students receive specific feedback from the teacher on their work.
- The teacher does not complete the lesson as planned. She makes certain that all students are able to justify their answers before moving on.
- The teacher records student levels as she works with them.

Record of Evidence

Cluster 6: Professionalism

Guiding Questions

- *To what extent does the teacher engage with the professional community (within the school and beyond) and demonstrate a commitment to ongoing professional learning?*

- *Does the teacher collaborate productively with colleagues and contribute to the life of the school?*

- *Does the teacher engage in professional learning and take a leadership role in the school to promote the welfare of students?*

Evidence

No evidence of Cluster 6 is present in this Instructional Set.

**Looking at Teaching Through
the Lens of the FFT Clusters**

A Study Guide for
Teacher
Learning Communities

Teacher: Roberts
Subject: Social Studies
Grade: 11
Topic: Close Reading

Welcome to the Study Guide for the Roberts Social Studies Instructional Set, a collection of artifacts and videos for an instructional lesson. This Study Guide provides information and instructions on how to examine teaching and learning through the lens of the Framework for Teaching (FFT) Clusters. In order to complete the steps in this Guide, you will need access to the teacher's planning documents, the lesson video, and the teacher commentary video (http://www.danielsongroup.org/study-guides/). This Study Guide has been designed so Steps 1–5 focus on examining the Instructional Set and can be done by an individual. Step 6 is a group activity and focuses on proposed interactions with the featured teacher and applications of learning.

Step 1 - Lesson Overview

Read the background information of the lesson provided below.

This video is a good example of Close Reading and how you could use it in a classroom. The lesson integrates Social Studies and ELA. This lesson is the first of several days. Students are working in small groups, and each group has high, medium, and lower level students, who are grouped purposefully by the teacher. She states that this lesson is at a high level of inquiry and that is why she has chosen her groups, so the stronger students can lead the others. Also, the lower achieving students can use the concrete answers, while the others will also use inference. (This is indicated in the lesson plan.) The teacher also uses whole group instruction.

This is Day One of a three-day lesson. She begins the lesson with a probing question, "Why did the author use this?" The teacher notes pertinent vocabulary, and students answer questions citing evidence with the corresponding line numbers from the text throughout the video. Most students participate willingly, both within the whole group and in their smaller groups. They will ask if they are not sure of a vocabulary word. The teacher makes personal references to help students understand what they have read (e.g., teacher clarifies the "term talcum powder," relating it to changing a diaper).

Teacher uses formative assessment as she goes from group to group, checking written text evidence and student responses during the lesson.

Lesson objectives cited:
- Students will be able to read, speak, and write about a complex text.
- Students will be able to cite evidence from the text that supports a claim.
- Students will be able to discuss the text in small group and whole class settings.
- Students will understand the reasons why women wanted the right to vote.

Step 2 - Preparation and Questions

- *Read the teacher's lesson plan and jot down the key things you expect to see and what you want to look for in the video of the lesson.*
- *Write down any questions or comments you have about the lesson plan.*

Step 3 – Viewing the Classroom Video

- *Watch the video of the entire lesson, noting those things you expected to see based on the lesson plan.*
- *Note what was missing based on your expectations from the lesson plan. Jot down significant behaviors of the teacher and students pertinent to the FFT Clusters.*
- *After watching the video, look at the samples of student work provided (if available).*

Step 4 – Selected Highlights of the Lesson Video

Read the highlights of the lesson provided below. Note those matching your highlights of the lesson. Add the highlights of note you selected in Step 3 to this list. For each set of statements, determine the FFT Cluster that is best related to the behaviors presented.

> A. The teacher uses the student's level of ability in determining who will be in which group. She states that this is to get diversity of thought. Students have few if any questions about their assignment/task. (Cluster ___)
>
> B. The interaction between the teacher and students seems very positive. The teacher uses humor to get her point across. She does not tell any student they were incorrect, but does lead them with questions to come to a better conclusion. (Cluster ___)
>
> C. The teacher moves from group to group, insisting that the members of the group persevere through the questions. The teacher makes analogies to support students in their understanding of vocabulary words; this encourages them to persevere and work hard. (Cluster ___)

D. The teacher handles minor behavior problems with humor, correcting the problems with no class disruption. The procedures for getting attention and for getting into their Google docs are smooth; there is little to no loss of instruction time. (Cluster ___)

E. Most students are intellectually engaged during the lesson, although some students do not work intently unless the teacher is present. However, the students can give exact lines to support their claim when called upon. (Cluster ___)

F. Student understanding is primarily by asking questions and recording answers for others to see. The teacher's feedback to students is often global ("fantastic, nice job"), while at other times she gives specific input into what she needs to see in the group's responses. (Cluster ___)

G. Based on the student work provided, the students seem to have understood the main objectives of the lesson. (Cluster ___)

Step 5 – Viewing the Teacher Commentary

Watch the video of the teacher's commentary about the lesson and jot down any questions or comments you have about the commentary. Read the highlights below and identify the related FFT Cluster.

A. The teacher states that the students will be reading *The Great Gatsby* in their English Language Arts class. She explains that this is the perfect time to be reading the text, "A Critique on America," as it will help the students understand the American people right after World War I. (Cluster ___)

B. She states that by using a Close Read, all students can participate and be successful. The lower ability students can use the literal information from the text, while the higher ability students can extrapolate information from the text. This makes a richer discussion for everyone. (Cluster ____)

C. The teacher states that this year she has been focusing on vocabulary. She says this helps them not only in her class but in other classes as well. (Cluster ____)

D. Ms. Roberts states that part of the reason this lesson was successful was due to her continual circulation in the room. She says that she likes to go from small group to large group. This allows her to see where her students are without grading every paper. (Cluster ____)

E. She states that one of the things that was very successful was her groupings. "I was able to put kids together who were friends, while still having stronger students with weaker students. (Cluster ____)

Step 6 – Questions, Applications, and Discussion

The purpose of this step is to prompt your analysis and reflection of the Instructional Set and to have you think about applications to your own practice.

1. **Teaching and Learning Related to the FFT Clusters**

The purpose of the activity is to increase your understanding of the relationship between the highlights of the Instructional Set and the FFT Clusters. Your identification of an FFT Cluster for each of the highlights is compared to the Cluster identified by the master coders. The Answer Key is located at the end of the activities. You have options on how to complete the comparison. Determine what might work best for your group's learning. Options include, but are not limited to the following.

- Look at the first set of highlights. Take a poll of what each group member identified as the related FFT Cluster. If all members said the same FFT Cluster, have one or two members say why. Compare the group's response to the answer sheet. Repeat for the remainder of the highlights.

OR

- Have each member take one or two highlights. State the correct answer for each one, and a reason why the highlight demonstrates that FFT Cluster. The member will facilitate a discussion if others had different responses, with the goal of having all understand the justification of the correct answer.

OR

- Have members check their own responses to all the highlights. If there are any incorrect answers, then the member selects one highlight and leads a discussion with the group to learn why others think the highlight matches the correct FFT Cluster.

OR

- Determine your own process to check and discuss the match between highlights and the FFT Clusters.

2. **Analysis and Reflection of the Instructional Set**

The purpose of this activity is for you to analyze and reflect on what you saw and heard in the artifacts and videos, to share your analysis with your peers, and to discuss some of the questions or comments you noted. Review the notes, comments, and questions you recorded when you examined the Instructional Set.

- Identify a key teaching and learning attribute demonstrated in the Instructional Set that was effective and state why you think it worked well.
- Identify a different attribute and provide ideas about how it could be enhanced or improved.
- Share your statements with your group and have your peers react to and build upon your analysis and ideas.

Sample statements:

Ms. Roberts, when one student started talking with the Queen of England accent, you stated that it is important to be flexible because you can't always prepare for that kind of behavior. What goes on in your head during times like these so that you can remain flexible?

Ms. Roberts, you said that it was important to go between small group and large group instruction. What do you pay attention to that lets you know when to go back to large group and to write answers on the elmo?

3. **Notice, Learn, and Apply**

The purpose of this activity is for you to reflect on what you learned from your analysis of the Instructional Set, and to determine how you will apply it to your teaching.

- Complete the statements:
  "I noticed _____."
  (Insert one thing you noticed about the teacher or students.)

  "And I learned _____."
  (State what you learned related to what you noticed.)

"I will apply what I learned by _____ ."
(Provide example of how you will use what you learned in your own context.)

- Share your statements with your group. Have others react and also add how they might apply what you noticed to their own teaching context.

Sample statements:

I noticed that you moved from small group to large group several times throughout this lesson.

I learned that this kept the students focused on completing the task with their group.

I will apply what I've learned by creating criteria around when to move from small group to large group.

Alternative Step 6 Activity:

1. **Analysis and Reflection of the Instructional Set**
The purpose of this activity is for you to analyze and reflect on what you saw and/or heard in the artifacts and videos that relate to problems of practice that you might be facing or have faced in the past.

- Your Professional Learning Team has just watched this video. What FFT clusters stand out for you within this video?
- Prepare some statements you might want to bring to a meeting. These statements might include a key teaching and learning attribute that was demonstrated, something

you felt was highly successful, or an area where you might have a question.

- Share your statements with your group and have your peers react to and build upon your ideas.

Sample statements:

Throughout this lesson I noticed how Ms. Roberts used humor. I'm often afraid to use humor for fear my students will get completely off task and I won't be able to pull them back in. I'm wondering how others successfully use humor in their classrooms.

I noticed that Ms. Roberts gave global feedback to students as she was walking around. I struggle with this as well. What are some strategies you (the PLC) have used to give specific feedback to students during work time as demonstrated during the video?

2. **Notice, Learn, and Apply**

The purpose of this activity is for you to reflect on what you learned from your analysis of the Instructional Set and to determine how you might apply it to your own teaching.

- Complete the statements:
"I noticed _____."
(Insert one thing you noticed about the teacher or students.)

"And I learned _____."
(State what you learned related to what you noticed.)

"I will apply what I learned by _____."
(Provide example of how you will use what you learned in your own context.)

- Share your statements with your group. Have others react and also add how they might apply what you noticed to their own teaching context.

Sample statements:

I noticed that Ms. Roberts gave global feedback as she was roaming the room.

I learned several different strategies that my colleagues use while they are circulating (e.g., you share a specific example from the text, along with your extrapolation of what this might mean).

I will use this with my students as they read... .

Study Guide for Teachers Answer Key

Highlights from the
Lesson Video
(Step 4)

A. The teacher uses the student's level of ability in determining who will be in which group. She states that this is to get diversity of thought. Students have few if any questions about their assignment/task. (Cluster 1 Clarity of Instructional Purpose and Accuracy of Content)

B. The interaction between the teacher and students seems very positive. The teacher uses humor to get her point across. She does not tell any student they were incorrect, but does lead them with questions to come to a better conclusion. (Cluster 2 Safe, Respectful, Supportive, and Challenging Learning Environment)

C. The teacher moves from group to group, insisting that the members of the group persevere through the questions. The teacher makes analogies to support students in their understanding of vocabulary words; this encourages them to persevere and work hard. (Cluster 2 Safe, Respectful, Supportive, and Challenging Learning Environment)

D. The teacher handles minor behavior problems with humor, correcting the problems with no class disruption. The procedures for getting attention and for getting into their Google docs are smooth; there is little to no loss of instruction time. (Cluster 3 Classroom Management)

E. Most students are intellectually engaged during the lesson, although some students do not work intently unless the teacher is present. However, the students can give exact lines to support their claim when called upon. (Cluster 4 Student Intellectual Engagement)

F. Student understanding is primarily by asking questions and recording answers for others to see. The teacher's feedback to students is often global ("fantastic, nice job"), while at other times she gives specific input into what she needs to see in the group's responses. (Cluster 5 Successful Learning for All Students

G. Based on the student work provided, the students seem to have understood the main objectives of the lesson. (Cluster 5 Successful Learning for All Students

Study Guide for Teachers Answer Key

Highlights from the
Teacher Commentary
(Step 5)

A. The teacher states that the students will be reading *The Great Gatsby* in their English Language Arts class. She explains that this is the perfect time to be reading the text, "A Critique on America," as it will help the students understand the American people right after World War I. (Cluster 1 Clarity of Instructional Purpose and Accuracy of Content)

B. She states that by using a Close Read, all students can participate and be successful. The lower ability students can use the literal information from the text, while the higher ability students can extrapolate information from the text. This makes a richer discussion for everyone. (Cluster 1 Clarity of Instructional Purpose and Accuracy of Content)

C. The teacher states that this year she has been focusing on vocabulary. She says this helps them not only in her class but in other classes as well. (Cluster 1 Clarity of Instructional Purpose and Accuracy of Content)

D. Ms. Roberts states that part of the reason this lesson was successful was due to her continual circulation in the room. She says that she likes to go from small group to large group. This allows her to see where her students are without grading every paper. (Cluster 5 Successful Learning by All Students)

E. She states that one of the things that was very successful was her groupings. "I was able to put kids together who were friends, while still having stronger students with weaker students. (Teacher reflection on Cluster 2 Safe, Respectful, Supportive, and Challenging Learning Environment)

**Looking at Teaching Through
the Lens of the FFT Clusters**

A Study Guide for
Instructional Coach
Learning Communities

Teacher: Roberts
Subject: Social Studies
Grade: 11
Topic: Close Reading

Welcome to the Study Guide for the Roberts Social Studies Instructional Set, a collection of artifacts and videos for an instructional lesson. This Study Guide provides information and instructions on how to examine teaching and learning through the lens of the Framework for Teaching (FFT) Clusters. In order to complete the steps in this Guide, you will need access to the teacher's planning documents, the lesson video, and the teacher commentary video (http://www.danielsongroup.org/study-guides/). This Study Guide has been designed so Steps 1–5 focus on examining the Instructional Set, and can be done by an individual. Step 6 is a group activity and focuses on proposed interactions with the featured teacher and on applications of learning.

Step 1 - Lesson Overview

Read the background information of the lesson provided below.

This video is a good example of Close Reading and how you could use it in a classroom. The lesson integrates Social Studies and ELA. This lesson is the first of several days. Students are working in small groups, and each group has high, medium, and lower level students, who are grouped purposefully by the teacher. She states that this lesson is at a high level of inquiry and that is why she has chosen her groups, so the stronger students can lead the others. Also, the lower achieving students can use the concrete answers, while the others will also use inference. (This is indicated in the lesson plan.) The teacher also uses whole group instruction.

This is Day One of a three-day lesson. She begins the lesson with a probing question, "Why did the author use this?" The teacher notes pertinent vocabulary, and students answer questions citing evidence with the corresponding line numbers from the text throughout the video. Most students participate willingly, both within the whole group and in their smaller groups. They will ask if they are not sure of a vocabulary word. The teacher makes personal references to help students understand what they have read (e.g., teacher clarifies the "term talcum powder," relating it to changing a diaper).

Teacher uses formative assessment as she goes from group to group, checking written text evidence and student responses during the lesson.

Lesson objectives cited:
- Students will be able to read, speak, and write about a complex text.
- Students will be able to cite evidence from the text that supports a claim.
- Students will be able to discuss the text in small group and whole class settings.
- Students will understand the reasons why women wanted the right to vote.

Step 2 - Preparation and Questions

- *Read the teacher's lesson plan and jot down the key things you expect to see and what you want to look for in the video of the lesson.*
- *Write down any questions or comments you have about the lesson plan.*

Step 3 – Viewing the Classroom Video

- *Watch the video of the entire lesson, noting those things you expected to see based on the lesson plan.*

- *Note what was missing based on your expectations from the lesson plan. Jot down significant behaviors of the teacher and students pertinent to the FFT Clusters.*

- *After watching the video, look at the samples of student work provided (if available).*

Step 4 – Selected Highlights of the Lesson Video

Read the highlights of the lesson provided below. Note those matching your highlights of the lesson. Add the highlights of note you selected in Step 3 to this list. For each set of statements, determine the FFT Cluster that is best related to the behaviors presented.

A. The teacher uses the student's level of ability in determining who will be in which group. She states that this is to get diversity of thought. Students have few if any questions about their assignment/task. (Cluster ____)

B. The interaction between the teacher and students seems very positive. The teacher uses humor to get her point across. She does not tell any student they were incorrect, but does lead them with questions to come to a better conclusion. (Cluster ____)

C. The teacher moves from group to group, insisting that the members of the group persevere through the questions. The teacher makes analogies to support students in their understanding of vocabulary words; this encourages them to persevere and work hard. (Cluster ____)

D. The teacher handles minor behavior problems with humor, correcting the problems with no class disruption. The procedures for getting attention and for

---

getting into their Google docs are smooth; there is little to no loss of instruction time. (Cluster ___)

E. Most students are intellectually engaged during the lesson, although some students do not work intently unless the teacher is present. However, the students can give exact lines to support their claim when called upon. (Cluster ___)

F. Student understanding is primarily by asking questions and recording answers for others to see. The teacher's feedback to students is often global ("fantastic, nice job"), while at other times she gives specific input into what she needs to see in the group's responses. (Cluster ___)

G. Based on the student work provided, the students seem to have understood the main objectives of the lesson. (Cluster ___)

Step 5 – Viewing the Teacher Commentary

Watch the video of the teacher's commentary about the lesson and jot down any questions or comments you have about the commentary. Read the highlights below and identify the related FFT Cluster.

A. The teacher states that the students will be reading *The Great Gatsby* in their English Language Arts class. She explains that this is the perfect time to be reading the text, "A Critique on America," as it will help the students understand the American people right after World War I. (Cluster ___)

B. She states that by using a Close Read, all students can participate and be successful. The lower ability students can use the literal information from the text, while the higher ability students can extrapolate information from the text. This makes a richer discussion for everyone. (Cluster ___)

C. The teacher states that this year she has been focusing on vocabulary. She says this helps them not only in her class but in other classes as well. (Cluster ___)
D. Ms. Roberts states that part of the reason this lesson was successful was due to her continual circulation in the room. She says that she likes to go from small group to large group. This allows her to see where her students are without grading every paper. (Cluster ___)
E. She states that one of the things that was very successful was her groupings. "I was able to put kids together who were friends, while still having stronger students with weaker students. (Cluster ___)

Step 6 – Questions, Applications, and Discussion

The purpose of this step is to prompt your analysis of and reflection on the Instructional Set and to have you think about applications to your own practice.

1. **Preparation for professional conversation with the featured teacher**

Suppose you have the opportunity to talk with Ms. Roberts, one-on-one. Think about some questions you would like to ask her about the strategies used or decisions made for this Instructional Set.

- Prepare what you would say to her by providing a brief summary for context and your questions to get additional information. Think of your coaching strategies as you prepare your questions. Next, think of what you would say to her to prompt thinking about next steps to enhance her practice.

- Share your summaries and questions to elicit additional information with your group. Have your peers comment about your questions and add other questions they had about the same event you summarized. Take turns sharing and discussing the sets of questions

The purpose of this activity is to have you analyze and reflect on what you saw or heard in the artifacts and videos, and practice preparing questions to get more information about the teacher's thinking and the behaviors of both students and the teacher, which is one element of an instructional coaching session. Feedback about the questions should include to what extent they are appropriate and will obtain useful information without making the featured teacher feel uneasy or criticized. The second part of this activity focuses on helping teachers move their practice forward.

Sample A:

Ms. Roberts, I noticed that when you were roaming the room looking on group work, you made comments such as, "fantastic, nice job," while at other times you gave more specific input into what you needed to see in the group's responses. What were you paying attention to that led you to these two types of feedback?

Sample B:

Ms. Roberts, you said you had been working on increasing the students' vocabulary, not only for your class, but for other classes and for their future success as students. What criteria do you use to determine the vocabulary you want students to work on?

Sample C:

Ms. Roberts, your lesson includes the learning objective; 'Students will understand the reasons why women wanted the right to vote," yet none of their comments related to this objective. Knowing that this was day one of several days on this topic, to what degree was this an important learning objective for this lesson? What might you do to encourage students to address this learning objective?

2. **Notice, Learn, and Apply**

The purpose of this activity is for you to reflect on what you learned from your analysis of the Instructional Set and to determine how you will apply it to your coaching.

- Complete the statements:
  "I noticed _____."
  (Insert one thing you noticed about the teacher or students.)

  "And I learned _____."
  (State what you learned related to what you noticed.)

  "I will apply what I learned by _____."
  (Provide example of how you will use what you learned in your own context.)

- Share your statements with your group. Have others react and add how they might apply what you noticed to their own coaching context.

Sample statement:
- I noticed a potential area of growth: giving specific feedback to students.
- I learned that I can phrase questions around a potential area of growth without the question being accusatory.
- I will apply what I learned by writing out questions of potential areas of growth before a difficult conversation with a teacher.

Study Guide for Instructional Coaches Answer Key

Highlights from the
Lesson Video
(Step 4)

A. The teacher uses the student's level of ability in determining who will be in which group. She states that this is to get diversity of thought. Students have few if any questions about their assignment/task. (Cluster 1 Clarity of Instructional Purpose and Accuracy of Content)

B. The interaction between the teacher and students seems very positive. The teacher uses humor to get her point across. She does not tell any student they were incorrect, but does lead them with questions to come to a better conclusion. (Cluster 2 Safe, Respectful, Supportive, and Challenging Learning Environment)

C. The teacher moves from group to group, insisting that the members of the group persevere through the questions. The teacher makes analogies to support students in their understanding of vocabulary words; this encourages them to persevere and work hard. (Cluster 2 Safe, Respectful, Supportive, and Challenging Learning Environment)

D. The teacher handles minor behavior problems with humor, correcting the problems with no class disruption. The procedures for getting attention and for getting into their Google docs are smooth; there is little to no loss of instruction time. (Cluster 3 Classroom Management)

E. Most students are intellectually engaged during the lesson, although some students do not work intently unless the teacher is present. However, the students can give exact lines to support their claim when called upon. (Cluster 4 Student Intellectual Engagement)

F. Student understanding is primarily by asking questions and recording answers for others to see. The teacher's feedback to students is often global ("fantastic, nice job"), while at other times she gives specific input into what she needs to see in the group's responses. (Cluster 5 Successful Learning for All Students

G. Based on the student work provided, the students seem to have understood the main objectives of the lesson. (Cluster 5 Successful Learning for All Students

Study Guide for Instructional Coaches Answer Key

Highlights from the
Teacher Commentary
(Step 5)

A. The teacher states that the students will be reading *The Great Gatsby* in their English Language Arts class. She explains that this is the perfect time to be reading the text, "A Critique on America," as it will help the students understand the American people right after World War I. (Cluster 1 Clarity of Instructional Purpose and Accuracy of Content)

B. She states that by using a Close Read, all students can participate and be successful. The lower ability students can use the literal information from the text, while the higher ability students can extrapolate information from the text. This makes a richer discussion for everyone. (Cluster 1 Clarity of Instructional Purpose and Accuracy of Content)

C. The teacher states that this year she has been focusing on vocabulary. She says this helps them not only in her class but in other classes as well. (Cluster 1 Clarity of Instructional Purpose and Accuracy of Content)

D. Ms. Roberts states that part of the reason this lesson was successful was due to her continual circulation in the room. She says that she likes to go from small group to large group. This allows her to see where her students are without grading every paper. (Cluster 5 Successful Learning by All Students)

E. She states that one of the things that was very successful was her groupings. "I was able to put kids together who were friends, while still having stronger students with weaker students. (Teacher reflection on Cluster 2 Safe, Respectful, Supportive, and Challenging Learning Environment)

Record of Evidence

This Record of Evidence (ROE) contains key evidence aligned to the FFT Clusters. Interpretive statements about the evidence are also provided. The ROE was created by two master coders who recorded evidence and interpretation statements independently, reviewed each others' work, and arrived at a final composite version based on their professional conversations. This version was reviewed by a leader of the master coders. The ROE is included in this Study Guide so users can see what master coders identified as key evidence, and their interpretation of that evidence through the lens of the FFT Clusters. It is provided as an example of one type of analysis of an Instructional Set. The ROEs were created for professional development rather than evaluative purposes. Users are cautioned about using them for teacher evaluation.

Rubric:	Generic
Grade:	11th
Subject:	Social Studies
Topic:	Close Reading
Teacher description:	Female, caucasian, 9 years experience
Class description:	Approximately 26+ students; diverse ethnic groups; seems to be a higher-level history class. Students are grouped with high, medium, and lower level students in each group. Fifty minute class period.
Artifacts:	• Lesson Plan • Teacher Commentary • Class materials (article students read) • Student work samples • Instructional Coaching Guide - noted, but not coded
Length of video:	37:39

Record of Evidence

Cluster 1: Clarity of Instructional Purpose and Accuracy of Content

Guiding Questions

- *To what extent does the teacher demonstrate depth of important content knowledge and conduct the class with a clear and ambitious purpose, reflective of the standards for the discipline and appropriate to the students' levels of knowledge and skill?*

- *To what degree are the elements of a lesson (the sequence of topics, instructional strategies, and materials and resources) well designed and executed, and aligned with the purpose of the lesson?*

- *To what extent are they designed to engage students in high-level learning in the discipline?*

Evidence

Instructional Plan
- The lesson plan is comprehensive and the description of the activities and lesson objectives state:
  - Students will be able to read, speak, and write about a complex text.
  - Students will be able to cite evidence from the text that supports a claim.
  - Students will be able to discuss the text in small group and whole class settings.
  - Students will understand the reasons why women wanted the right to vote.
- The teacher cites CCSS from the History standard: "explain the major social, technological, and cultural developments of the 1920's."
- The teacher incorporates both Social Studies and Language Arts, using inference, figurative language, opinions based on evidence from the text, and active listening.
- Close Reading steps as outlined in the Lesson Plan.
- Teacher places students in small specific groups (each group contains high, medium, and lower academic level students).
- Teacher will use formative assessment as she goes from group to group, checking on student responses during the lesson, and the evidence the students write from text sources.
- This lesson seems to be at a high level of inquiry. She has chosen her groups so the stronger students can lead. Lower achieving students can use concrete answers; others will also use inference.
- The lesson plan has a definite structure, with timings allotted to each of the parts of the lesson. During the video of this lesson, the teacher holds true to the time frames, and for most students it is adequate time.
- The lesson plan indicates a final assessment, but no means to formatively assess throughout the days of the plan. There are no criteria for the quality of the paragraph to be turned in. The teacher does include minimal student work with the plan.

Record of Evidence

Cluster 1: Clarity of Instructional Purpose and Accuracy of Content

Evidence (cont'd.)

- There is an error on the handout; however, the teacher caught it and referred to it in the post-observation commentary.

Lesson Video

- Teacher says this is a "cold read" and students must read this 2-3 times to accomplish the tasks assigned.
- This is day one of a three-day lesson. The teacher follows her lesson plan for day one. She begins the video with a probing question, "Why did the author use this?"
- Students answer questions, citing evidence and line numbers. Most students volunteer.
- Teacher made some personal references to a student to get an idea across. Teacher uses academic language.
- Students seem to relate to teacher's use of humor in the lesson.
- New vocabulary is noted .The teacher is able to describe what vocabulary words mean in a manner that students understand. Example: talcum powder, relating it to changing a diaper. Teacher talks about concrete vs. non-concrete.

Teacher Commentary

- Teacher understands how the CCSS support the content of History.
- Teacher reads the core actions, then gives a rationale for why this lesson fits these core actions.
- Teacher explains how she was fortunate to have the time to find a document that meets the standards.
- She talks about how her teaching has moved from being very teacher-directed to more student-directed. She does not give specifics, just that students can surprise you.
- T: Multiple levels of readers offers more multiple perspectives during these lessons. This is very important.
- T: I was amazed at the number of places they found references for their answers. She states several specific examples.

Record of Evidence

Cluster 1:   **Clarity of Instructional Purpose and Accuracy of Content**

Interpretation
- We see objectives for all days in this lesson plan. In the video, we see only day one, so we don't know if all objectives are met.
- The lesson combines Social Studies and Language Arts.
- Students all seem engaged in the activity. Most want to add to the discussion, indicating they understand what they are to do.
- Teacher shares personal things with class.
- A coherent sequence of questions, used in the lesson plan, is carried out in the lesson.
- There is an error on the handout. 1820 is used instead of the correct 1920, but the teacher caught it, and mentions that it shows that teachers do make mistakes. She did say she would proofread one more time, when using handouts.
- The teacher definitely understands how the CCSS can be integrated into the content of history. She understands that a Close Read promotes students' learning and engagement, rather than the teacher being the disseminator of knowledge.
- There is nothing in the plan or the accompanying documents that indicates what quality looks like in the eye of the teacher, nor what the teacher is actually looking for in response to the objective; e.g., why did women want the right to vote?
- The teacher uses the student's level of ability in determining who will be in which group and she states that this is to get diversity of thought.

Record of Evidence

Cluster 2: Safe, Respectful, Supportive, and Challenging Learning Environment

Guiding Questions

- *To what extent do the interactions between teacher and students, and among students, demonstrate genuine caring and a safe, respectful, supportive, and also challenging learning environment?*

- *Do teachers convey high expectations for student learning and encourage hard work and perseverance? Is the environment safe for risk taking?*

- *Do students take pride in their work and demonstrate a commitment to mastering challenging content?*

Evidence

- Teacher uses humor to get her point across: "That was a doozie."
- T: Great reasons. Fantastic, great job.
- Student asks about Zion, teacher sings from a song using the word. T: That's my best Bob Marley.
- Teacher shares personal information. T: No I won't take you to the zoo; Mr. Roberts is a teacher too.
- Students and teacher seem to have a good rapport and mutual respect.
- The teacher demonstrates knowledge and caring about individual students' lives beyond school. T: What is an idea? Like when you liked that boy last year—ideas change.
- Students share their ideas and opinions with each other and use the text and line numbers to back up their thoughts.
- Students don't seem to be afraid to share with the whole class and their group.
- Students will ask if they are not sure of a vocabulary word.
- The students are productively and collaboratively engaged during small group work.
- Teacher uses students names. T: Roosevelt, get those headphones off your noggin.
- Teacher continually asks probing questions to get students thinking.
- T: As I walk around I see line numbers and concepts.
- The teacher continually walks from group to group, checking on progress and for questions and comments.
- T: What I want accomplished….
- For closure, the teacher does a whole class session answering the questions on the ELMO.
- The teacher gives the assignment for the next day.
- T: Do your work so I can do mine.
- Teacher uses an ELMO to write responses from students.
- T: All right, jump in on this, don't make me call your name.

Record of Evidence

Cluster 2: Safe, Respectful, Supportive, and Challenging Learning Environment

Evidence (cont'd.)

- Teacher gives the example of putting baby powder on a baby. S: Thank you Miss Roberts.
- T: Come on, get everyone in on the love.
- 22:42: Teacher stays with 3 students to get them to persevere through the questions.
- T: Knock, knock. S: Who's there? T: The back of the page.
- T: You can squeak at me, but that is not going to make it go away.
- T: Be good, be smart, behave.

Interpretation
- The interaction between the teacher and students seems very positive.
- The teacher uses humor to get her point across. She does not tell any student they were incorrect, but led them with questions to a better conclusion.
- The teacher does seem to know about individual students' lives outside of school.
- The teacher seems to enjoy this class.
- The interactions between the teacher and the students are respectful, playful, and supportive.
- The teacher moves from group to group, insisting that the members of the group persevere through the questions.
- The teacher makes analogies to support students in their understanding of vocabulary words; this encourages them to persevere and work hard.

Record of Evidence

Cluster 3:   Classroom Management

Guiding Questions

- *Is the classroom well run and organized?*

- *Are classroom routines and procedures clear and carried out efficiently by both teacher and students with little loss of instructional time?*

- *To what extent do students themselves take an active role in their smooth operation?*

- *Are directions for activities clearly explained so that there is no confusion?*

- *Do students not only understand and comply with standards of conduct, but also play an active part in setting the tone for maintaining those standards?*

- *How does the physical environment support the learning activities?*

Evidence

- Students are seated in groups to facilitate their group work. It is easy for the teacher to walk from group to group, and for the students to see the whiteboard. The students seem to know what to do and there is little loss of instructional time.
- The class is very well run for the most part, with little student misbehavior. The teacher again uses humor to get her point across to Roosevelt.
- T: What do you have on your noggin? Later, T: Roosevelt if you don't get those headphones off your noggin….
- T: Titus, you get one and then you are done.
- The teacher continually monitors student behavior.
- Uses 3-2-1 to get the class's attention. T: Give me 3-2-1.
- There is much displayed on the walls of the classroom. One is a picture of students.
- T: Finger on your nose if you need a little info on what is talcum powder?
- Teacher monitors behavior and understanding by walking around.

Interpretation
- Desks are arranged to facilitate group work. Students can see their classmates' faces when they are speaking.
- Worksheets are passed out as the teacher is speaking to the students to give directions.
- The teacher handles minor behavior problems with humor, which corrects the problems with no class disruption.
- The procedures for getting attention and for getting into their Google docs are smooth and there is little to no loss of instruction time.
- Students have few/if any questions about their assignment/task.

Record of Evidence

Cluster 4: Student Intellectual Engagement

Guiding Questions

- *To what extent are students intellectually engaged in a classroom of high intellectual energy?*

- *What is the nature of what students are doing?*

- *Are they being challenged to think and make connections through both the instructional activities and the questions explored?*

- *Do the teacher's explanations of content correctly model academic language and invite intellectual work by students?*

- *Are students asked to explain their thinking, to construct logical arguments citing evidence, and to question the thinking of others?*

- *Are the instructional strategies used by the teacher suitable to the discipline, and to what extent do they promote student agency in the learning of challenging content?*

Evidence

- Students are reading, interpreting, discussing, listening, and supporting their statements with evidence from the text, citing the evidence and line number.
- The teacher questions the students
  - T: What does that mean? Why do you think that? Where did you find that?
  - T: What's a symbol you use every day? (She then explains how that connects to the question.)
  - T: What would indicate to you that they are childish?
  - T: Give me some specifics.
- The teacher uses wait time, allowing a student to read through her notes to find the best answer and the evidence to support that answer.
- The teacher uses both whole group discussion and small group work, and monitors the groups as she circulates around the room.
- The teacher has provided a worksheet with high-level questions as well as questions that have concrete answers to provide some scaffolding.
- The teacher has students highlight vocabulary words. If students have trouble with them, she often gives examples of their meanings, using ideas that are familiar to students.
- The teacher summarizes the lesson by writing answers on her sheet, using the white board so all can see. Teacher calls on individual students for responses that she then writes on the paper shown by the ELMO.
- The teacher gives the homework assignment for the next day and says, "Do your work so I can do mine."

Record of Evidence

Cluster 4:   **Student Intellectual Engagement**

Interpretation
- Students are asked to cite evidence and line numbers to back up their answers.
- All students are actively engaged and give each other ideas they may not have thought about.
- Vocabulary is stressed.
- The teacher seems very enthusiastic; consequently, the students seem to be actively engaged and on task.
- Most students are intellectually engaged during the lesson, although some students do not work intently unless the teacher is present. When called upon, however, the students can give exact lines to support their claim.

Record of Evidence

Cluster 5:   Successful Learning by All Students
Guiding Questions

- *To what extent does the teacher ensure learning by all students?*

- *Does the teacher monitor student understanding through specifically designed questions or instructional techniques?*

- *To what extent do students monitor their own learning and provide respectful feedback to classmates?*

- *Does the teacher make modifications in presentations or learning activities where necessary, taking into account the degree of student learning?*

- *Has the teacher sought out other resources (including parents) to support students' learning?*

- *In reflection, is the teacher aware of the success of the lesson in reaching students?*

Evidence

Teacher Commentary
- T: Students learning with each other help social skills.
- T: When I let go, students flourish.
- T: Using figurative language and concrete language helps both higher and lower level students to succeed.
- The teacher states she has a writing assignment after each lesson to assess her students' learning.
- The teacher feels she has accomplished the objectives listed in her lesson plan.

Artifacts
- Looking at student work, most students accomplished the objectives on Close Reading.

Lesson video
- Student interactions during the discussions are respectful.
- The teacher uses formative assessment as she walks around and has a discussion with each group.
- The teacher assigns homework: to write in paragraph form, in proficiency style, an argument for or against Mencken's claim that the US is a four-ring circus. T: I need three pieces of evidence and your reasoning to justify your argument.
- The teacher walks around the classroom as students work, listening to their conversations, asking questions to deepen their understanding.
- T: Fantastic, make sure you add that and go on to #6.
- S: Can we use this last one? T: I think that's better used for a later question.
- T: Make sure you don't just tell me the numbers.

Record of Evidence

Cluster 5:   Successful Learning by All Students

Evidence (cont'd.)

- T: I can totally understand where you're going with that.
- T: Give me some specifics, what did the common man enjoy?
- T: Nice job getting into it.

Interpretation
- The teacher has a summative method for evaluating each day's lesson.
- Based on the student work provided, the students seem to have gotten the main objectives of the lesson.
- The teacher is constantly moving around the classroom, taking the pulse of their learning.
- Assessing student understanding is primarily done by asking questions and then recording them for others to see.
- The teacher's feedback to students is often global, "fantastic, nice job" etc., but at other times, she gives specific input into what she needs to see in the group's responses.

Record of Evidence

Cluster 6:   Professionalism

Guiding Questions

- *To what extent does the teacher engage with the professional community (within the school and beyond) and demonstrate a commitment to ongoing professional learning?*

- *Does the teacher collaborate productively with colleagues and contribute to the life of the school?*

- *Does the teacher engage in professional learning and take a leadership role in the school to promote the welfare of students?*

Evidence

No evidence of Cluster 6 is present in this Instructional Set.

FFT Clusters Study Guide: Set 1 (Social Studies 11)

Appendix A: The FFT Clusters Study Guide Series Team

Ron Anderson, EdD; OH. Danielson Group Consultant.

Dauna Easley, MEd; OH. University of Cincinnati supervisor for student teachers.

Nancy Flickinger, MEd; OH. National Board Certified (AYA/ELA), Teaching Professions Academy Instructor.

Linda Goodwin, MEd; AR. Arkansas LEADS/TESS Support Consultant, Arkansas School Improvement Specialist, Arkansas Quest Leadership Mentor for Administrators, Danielson Group Consultant.

Bobbie Grice, MEd; OH. Resident Educator Coordinator.

Shirley Hall, MEd; NJ. President, GreenLight for Learning, LLC; Former School and District Administrator, Danielson Group Member.

Donna Hanby, PhD; OH. Educational Consultant (Assessment & Accreditation): Educator Preparation Programs.

Kathleen Hanson, MEd; ID. Hanson Educational Consulting, Danielson Group Consultant.

MaryLou McGirr, MEd; SD. Learning Specialist, Technology & Innovation in Education; Trainer for Cognitive Coaching; Danielson Group Consultant.

Joanie Peterson, MEd; OR. Human Resources/ Professional Development Administrator; Danielson Group Consultant.

Sue Presler, MEd; NE. Training Associate, Thinking Collaborative. Trainer for Cognitive Coaching, Adaptive Schools, and Habits of Mind, Danielson Group Member.

Carol Rauch, EdD; OH. University of Cincinnati supervisor for student teachers and Associate Director of Professional Development; Danielson Group Consultant.

Cynthia M. Tocci, PhD; VA. Educational Observations, LLC, Danielson Group Director of Instructional Design.

Appendix B:
List of Study Guide Sets

Set No.	Subject	Grade
1	ELA	8
	Math	3
	Social Studies	11
2	Tech	9
	ELA	8
	Math	4
3	Math	9-10
	ELA	2
	Social Studies	7
4	ELA	12
	Math	2
	Social Studies	9
5	Science & Tech	4
	Math	11
	ELA	7
6	Math	10
	ELA	5
	Math	K
7	Math	6
	ELA	9
	Math	1
8	ELA	K
	ELA	4
	Math	9

THE
DANIELSON
GROUP

Vision

Each educator and student experiences a safe and inclusive learning environment that promotes joyful inquiry, efficacy, intellectual rigor, and reflection grounded in the Framework for Teaching.

Mission

To advance the principles of the Framework for Teaching by partnering with educators and policy leaders at all levels to strengthen professional practices and promote education policies that elevate teacher development and leadership in service of student learning.

For information about our services, or to download a free copy of the FFT Clusters document, visit our website: www.danielsongroup.org

Made in the USA
Coppell, TX
30 October 2019

10732360R00085